Building an eBusiness

From the Ground Up

Elizabeth Eisner Reding

Nerdsworth Computer Solutions
Gallup, New Mexico

McGraw-Hill
Irwin

Boston Burr Ridge, IL Dubuque, IA Madison, WI New York San Francisco St. Louis
Bangkok Bogotá Caracas Lisbon London Madrid
Mexico City Milan New Delhi Seoul Singapore Sydney Taipei Toronto

McGraw-Hill Higher Education

*A Division of The **McGraw-Hill** Companies*

BUILDING AN EBUSINESS: FROM THE GROUND UP
Published by McGraw-Hill/Irwin, an imprint of The McGraw-Hill Companies, Inc. 1221 Avenue of the Americas, New York, NY, 10020. Copyright © 2001, by The McGraw-Hill Companies, Inc. All rights reserved. No part of this publication may be reproduced or distributed in any form or by any means, or stored in a data base or retrieval system, without the prior written consent of The McGraw-Hill Companies, Inc., including, but not limited to, in any network or other electronic storage or transmission, or broadcast for distance learning.
Some ancillaries, including electronic and print components, may not be available to customers outside the United States.

This book is printed on acid-free paper.

1 2 3 4 5 6 7 8 9 0 QPD/QPD 0 9 8 7 6 5 4 3 2 1 0

ISBN   0-07-242636-5

Publisher: *David Kendric Brake*
Senior sponsoring editor: *Jodi McPherson*
Developmental editor: *Erin Riley*
Senior marketing manager: *Jeff Parr*
Senior project manager: *Susan Trentacosti*
Senior production supervisor: *Michael R. McCormick*
Senior designer: *Kiera Cunningham/Laurie J. Entringer*
Supplement coordinator: *Elizabeth Hadala*
Cover design: *Kiera Cunningham*
Cover illustration: *© The Stock Illustration Source, Inc.*
Interior design: *Maureen McCutcheon*
Compositor: *Carlisle Communications, Ltd.*
Typeface: *10/12 Aster*
Printer: *Quebecor Printing Book Group/Dubuque*

Library of Congress Cataloging-in-Publication Data

Reding, Elizabeth Eisner.
    Building an eBusiness : from the ground up / Elizabeth Eisner Reding.
        p. cm.
    Includes index.
    ISBN 0-07-242636-5
    1. Electronic commerce. 2. Web sites—Design. I. Title: Building an electronic business. II. Title.

HF5548.32 .R43 2001
658.8′4—dc21

                                                        00-060067

www.mhhe.com

Starting a new book is always exciting, not to mention scary, overwhelming, and tension-filled. I highly recommend it for anyone who is a thrill-seeker!

While my name may appear on the cover, there are many people who toil diligently in the background and contribute to its success. These people receive none of the glory but deserve much of the recognition. Among them are Jodi McPherson, Erin Riley, Melissa Forte, Jeff Parr, Mike Junior, David Brake, Laura Healy, Susan Trentacosti, Alexandra Arnold, and Stephanie Daneels. Without all the members of the team, this book would remain a daydream, rather than a reality.

And of course, there's my family. My husband, Michael, and my mother put up with my silly schedules and impossible mood swings all for the sake of 'the book.' To them, I say *Thank you* and *I love you*.

About the Author

Elizabeth Eisner Reding has been authoring computer books since 1993, and has written over 30 books. Most recently, she has written books on various Microsoft products (Excel, PowerPoint, and Publisher), Internet topics (such as HTML), and graphic art programs (Adobe Photoshop). She has also worked as a development editor and technical editor on many other computer books, and has published works with Course Technology, Microsoft Press, and Macmillan/Que.

Originally from New York State, Liz went to college at SUNY Binghamton, then moved to Boston, MA. After getting married (to a really terrific guy!), she and her husband moved to Santa Fe, New Mexico. Currently, they live in a small town on the Arizona/New Mexico border, close to the Navajo Nation.

Elizabeth Eisner Reding

To the Instructor and Student:

As we enter the 21st century, almost everything we do—work, school, home, leisure, and specifically business—will be affected and changed by the Web. With more change comes more opportunities, and these opportunities will lead us beyond traditional business and into what is now known as *eBusiness*. This book will help you combine the possibilities of the Internet with *business know-how* so that you can learn how to create your own opportunities within an eBusiness.

This book will help the budding entrepreneurs who want to begin an eBusiness but lack the rudimentary knowledge in the Internet and in developing business and marketing plans. By combining conceptual lessons with hands-on exercises, *Building an eBusiness* provides students with the opportunity to:

- Learn what is essential to build an eBusiness.
- Get hands-on training in specific eBusiness skills.
- Develop an understanding of eBusiness practices.

No business or computer knowledge is assumed, and within the concept of following individuals through various stages of developing an eBusiness—from idea inception to creating the company's web page—we have created an environment that is not only informative but also *interactive*.

Because print information becomes dated so quickly, we have also developed an extensive website—*http://www.mhhe.com/ebusiness*—to provide you with the most current content. The website will contain links to recent articles, relevant book reviews, and industry-recognized newsletters. We'll also offer success stories of .com companies and Internet entrepreneurs, with tips on how to be suc-

cessful in your own ventures. In addition, interactive exercises and additional problem solving situations will allow you to test the skills that you are learning in each chapter. With monthly updates, we will be able to give you most current information that you simply cannot get with just the book.

Whatever you do in business these days, you cannot escape the words eBusiness or eCommerce. The importance of these concepts—conducting business over the Internet—cannot be overemphasized, and most certainly cannot be ignored. The learning achieved within *Building an eBusiness* is the first tool you have to be a part of this constantly changing and ever-exciting new way of doing business.

Information Technology at McGraw-Hill/Irwin

At McGraw-Hill Higher Education, we publish instructional materials targeted at the higher education market. In an effort to expand the tools of higher learning, we publish texts, lab manuals, study guides, testing materials, software, and multimedia products.

At McGraw-Hill/Irwin (a division of McGraw-Hill Higher Education), we realize that technology has created and will continue to create new mediums for professors and students to use in managing resources and communicating information to one another. We strive to provide the most flexible and complete teaching and learning tools available as well as offer solutions to the changing world of teaching and learning.

 McGraw-Hill/Irwin is dedicated to providing the tools for today's instructors and students to successfully navigate the world of Information Technology.

- Seminar Series—McGraw-Hill/Irwin's Technology Connection seminar series offered across the country every year demonstrates the latest technology products and encourages collaboration among teaching professionals.

- McGraw-Hill/Osborne—This division of The McGraw-Hill Companies is known for its best-selling Internet titles, Harley Hahn's Internet & Web yellow pages, and the Internet Complete Reference.
- Digital Solutions—McGraw-Hill/Irwin is committed to publishing digital solutions. Taking your course online doesn't have to be a solitary adventure, nor does it have to be a difficult one. We offer several solutions that will allow you to enjoy all the benefits of having your course material online. For more information, visit Osborne at *www.osborne.com*.
- Packaging Options—For more information about our discount options, contact your McGraw-Hill/Irwin Sales representative at 1-800-338-3987 or visit our website at *www.mhhe.com/it*.

Resources for Instructors

We understand that, in today's teaching environment, offering a textbook alone is not sufficient to meet the needs of the many instructors who use our books. To teach effectively, instructors must have a full complement of supplemental resources to assist them in every facet of teaching from preparing for class, to conducting a lecture, to assessing students' comprehension. *Building an eBusiness* offers a complete, fully integrated supplements package and website, as described below.

Instructor's Resource Kit

- The Instructor's Resource Kit is a CD-ROM, containing the Instructor's Manual in both MS Word and .pdf formats, PowerPoint slides, Brownstone test generating software, and accompanying test item files for each chapter. The features of each component of the Instructor's Resource Kit are highlighted below.
- **Instructor's Manual:** The Instructor's manual contains a schedule showing how much time is required to cover the material in the chapter, a list of the chapter competencies and key terms, a Chapter Outline with lecture notes, a list of

numbered figures in the text, and suggested exercises. Also included are answers to all the exercises in the chapter review section and answers to On the Web exercises. The manual also contains a helpful introduction that explains the features, benefits, and suggested uses of the IM.

- **PowerPoint Presentation:** The PowerPoint presentation is designed to provide instructors with a comprehensive teaching resource that includes key terms and definitions, concept overviews, figures from the text, additional examples/illustrations, anticipated student questions with answers, and discussion topics. Included with the presentation are comprehensive speaker's notes.
- **Computerized Test Bank:** The test bank contains a series of questions categorized by topic and level of learning (definition, concept, and application). This same learning scheme is introduced in the website to provide a valuable testing and reinforcement tool. Each question is assigned a category: Level 1—definition, Level 2—concept, and Level 3—application. A test item table is provided for each chapter to give instructors a quick overview of the number and type of questions for each section in a chapter.

Digital Solutions to Help You Manage Your Course

- **PageOut**—PageOut is our Course Website Development Center that offers a syllabus page, URL, McGraw-Hill Online Learning Center content, online exercises and quizzes, gradebook, discussion board, and an area for student web pages.

  Available free with any McGraw-Hill/Irwin product, PageOut requires no prior knowledge of HTML, no long hours of coding, and a way for course coordinators and professors to provide a full-course website. PageOut offers a series of templates—simply fill them with your course information and click on one of 16 designs. The process takes under an hour and leaves you with a professionally designed website. We'll even get you started with sample websites, or enter your syllabus for you! PageOut is so straightforward and intuitive, it's little wonder why over 12,000 college professors are using it.

For more information, visit the PageOut website at: *www.pageout.net*.

- **Online Learning Centers/Websites**—The Online Learning Center (OLC) Website that accompanies *Building an eBusiness* is accessible through our Information Technology Supersite at *www.mhhe.com/it* or at the book site *www.mhhe.com/ebusiness*. This site provides additional learning and instructional tools developed using the same three-level approach found in the text and supplements to offer a consistent method for students to enhance their comprehension of the concepts presented in the text. The OLC/Website is divided into these three levels:

Level 1: Includes tips and tricks, FAQs, expanded book features such as "PC and You," and more *must know* items that interest students with and hyperlinks and extended examples.

Level 2: Includes additional quizzes for students to test their knowledge and skills. In our student focus groups across the country, students indicated this was a key piece of the website that increases their ability to be successful in class.

Level 3: Includes additional exercises and hands-on projects/activities in the following categories:

- Teamwork
- Ethics
- Buying a PC
- Privacy and Security
- Careers and the Impact of IT

- **Online Courses Available**—Online Learning Centers (OLCs) are your perfect solutions for Internet-based content. Simply put, these centers are "digital cartridges" that contain a book's pedagogy and supplements. As students read the book, they can go online and take self-grading quizzes or work through interactive exercises. These also provide students appropriate access to lecture materials and other key supplements. Online Learning Centers can be delivered through any of these platforms:

- McGraw-Hill Learning Architecture (TopClass)
- Blackboard.com

- Ecollege.com (formally Real Education)
- WebCT (a product of Universal Learning Technology)

McGraw-Hill has partnerships with **WebCT** and **Blackboard** to make it even easier to take your course online. Now you can have McGraw-Hill content delivered through the leading Internet-based learning tool for higher education.

At McGraw-Hill we have the following service agreements with **WebCT** and **Blackboard:**

Instructor Advantage

Instructor Advantage is a special level of service McGraw-Hill offers in conjunction with WebCT designed to help you get up and running with your new course. A team of specialists will be immediately available to ensure everything runs smoothly through the life of your adoption.

Instructor Advantage Plus

Qualified McGraw-Hill adopters will be eligible for an even higher level of service. A certified WebCT or Blackboard specialist will provide a full day of on-site training for you and your staff. You will then have unlimited e-mail and phone support through the life of your adoption. Please contact your local McGraw-Hill representative for more details.

Technology Connection Seminar Series

McGraw-Hill/Irwin's Technology Connection seminar series offered across the country every year demonstrates the latest technology products and encourages collaboration among teaching professionals.

MS Office 2000 Applications Texts and CDs

Available separately, or packaged with *Building an eBusiness*, McGraw-Hill offers three applications series: The O'Leary Series, The Advantage Series, or The Interactive Computing Series. Each series features its own unique approach to teaching MS Office to meet the needs of a variety of students and course goals.

- *The O'Leary Series* features a project-based, step-by-step walk-through of applications.
- *The Advantage Series* features a case-based, what, why and how approach to learning applications to enhance critical thinking skills.

- *The Interactive Computing Series* features a visual, two-page spread to provide a more skills-based approach to learning applications.

Each series offers Microsoft Office User Specialist (MOUS) approved courseware to signify that it has been independently reviewed and approved in complying with the standards of content coverage related to the Microsoft Exams and Certification Program. For more information on Microsoft's MOUS certification program, please visit Microsoft's website at *www.microsoft.com/office/traincert/*.

Also available for applications are the *Interactive Computing Series* Computer-Based Training CD-ROM tutorials. These CD-ROMs offer a visual, interactive way to develop and apply software skills. The CD-ROM features a unique "skills-concepts-steps" approach, and includes interactive exercises and performance-based assessment. These CD-ROMs are simulated, so there is no need for the actual software package on the computer.

Skills Assessment

McGraw-Hill/Irwin offers two innovative systems to meet your skills assessment needs. These two products are available for use with any of our applications manual series.

ATLAS (Active Technology Learning Assessment System) is one option to consider for an application skills assessment tool from McGraw-Hill. Atlas allows students to perform tasks while working live within the Microsoft applications environment. Atlas provides flexibility for you in your course by offering:

- Pre-testing options
- Post-testing options
- Course placement testing

- Diagnostic capabilities to reinforce skills
- Proficiency testing to measure skills
- ATLAS is web-enabled, customizable, and available for Microsoft Office 2000.

SimNet (Simulated Network Assessment Product)—SimNet is another option for a skills assessment tool that permits you to test students' software skills in a simulated environment. SimNet is available for Microsoft Office 97 (deliverable via a network) and Microsoft Office 2000 (deliverable via a network and the Web). SimNet provides flexibility for you in your course by offering:

- Pre-testing options
- Post-testing options
- Course placement testing
- Diagnostic capabilities to reinforce skills
- Proficiency testing to measure skills

For more information on either skills assessment software, please contact your local sales representative, or visit us at *www.mhhe.com/it*.

PowerWeb for eCommerce

PowerWeb is an exciting new online product available for *Building an eBusiness*. A nominally priced token grants students access through our website to a wealth of resources—all corresponding to eCommerce. Features include an interactive glossary; current events with quizzing, assessment, and measurement options; Web survey; links to related text content; and WWW searching capability via Northern Lights, an academic search engine.

Elizabeth Eisner Reding

CHAPTER 6

Developing

How Can I Enhance a Web Page?

So, you've created your website, but now you want to add features such as graphic images and hyperlinks that make your pages unique. Graphic images do more than just take up space; they say in an instant what you might need paragraphs to say. In a product-oriented eBusiness, you can use images of your products to enhance the site.

Using FrontPage, it is easy to add images. You can add links throughout your pages to make it simple for site visitors to jump to other related websites. Forms can be used to collect data from your site visitors. The data you collect can be helpful in your continuing marketing efforts and can help you improve your site.

Now that the Jewelry-For-You site has been created, Kim can spend some time making modifications that will enhance the site. It's already a good site: she just wants it to be better.

Opening Vignette

Each chapter begins with an *Opening Vignette* that places the upcoming chapter concepts and skills within a scenario so you can see when and how you need to apply these principles.

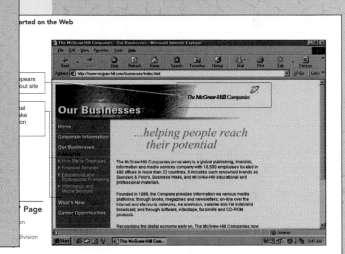

Take Note

When there is an explanation or concept that you should keep in mind, you will see a *Take Note*. These summaries provide helpful advisements and/or warnings that help ensure a smooth transition into your eBusiness.

Take Note
When you visit other websites, be aware of how certain elements affect you. Do you like particular colors or elements? Make a mental note of those features you'd like to incorporate into your own site. Be conscious of features you find irritating and want to avoid using.

What Makes for Good Web Pages?

It's not always that easy to describe what you like, but it's generally very easy to determine what you don't like. As you look through various pages, look not only at page content but also at design. Remember that you don't have to fit all your business information on a single page; spread the information out to many pages. For example, you might want a separate page to talk about your corporate vision, one for items you carry or services you provide, and one for any warranties that are available.

Several design principles found within good websites are:

- Readability, with an uncluttered look.
- Soothing, easy-to-read colors that don't distract from their content.
- Understandable wording that doesn't intimidate your readers.
- Navigation that enables your readers to easily get to pages within your site.
- Graphics that are small enough to easily download and enhance the site.
- Multimedia that adds value to the site.

What Is a Hyperlink?

One of the features that makes the Internet more than just a bunch of pretty pages is that you can jump from one page to another. This is accomplished through careful and deliberate planning of the site designer. Each time you click a link, or **hyperlink,** you are automatically taken to a different web page. Each hyperlink is an instruction to a new website, and this instruction contains an Internet address called a **URL (Uniform Resource Locator).** The default setting in many

The Edge

When there is a helpful hint that can make your new venture an easier or more successful one, you will find it located within *The Edge*.

FIGURE 3.11

Positioning Tips

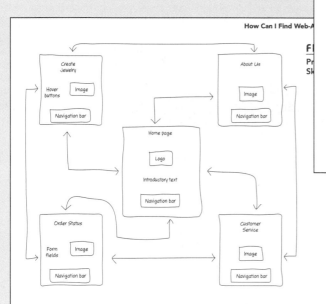

What Are My Marketing Tactics?

Understanding the strengths and weaknesses of your products or services makes it possible to develop a marketing strategy. Marketing strategies are based on **tactics**: the measures you take to make your strategies a reality. Marketing strategy questions are addressed in various websites, such as the one shown in Figure 3.12.

In marketing, there are a variety of tools at your disposal. Some of these tools are listed in the website shown in Figure 3.13.

What Should I Consider When Developing Marketing Tactics?

Before you can develop marketing tactics, you need to consider several factors that influence the current state of the market. These factors include the following:

- The size of the market, its growth potential, and the level of demand. This will also help you determine how you price your products or services.
- The availability of materials necessary to your business.
- Barriers to entry to you, your competitors, and your customers. Will it be difficult for you to get started in this business? Will it be difficult for your competitors to compete? Will it be easy for potential customers to begin working with you?
- The life cycle of your products or services. Can your products or services sustain growth and mature? Is the life cycle long enough that your business can recoup its investments? Do you have other products or services in the pipeline to augment or replace your current line? **Pipeline** is a metaphor for the process needed to bring a product or service from idea inception to reality.

THE EDGE

Depending on a single product or service is risky for any business. It's a good idea to always have a new product or service in the pipeline to replace or augment lackluster offerings. Additional offerings are a good hedge against a shift in the marketplace.

How Can I Find Web-A...

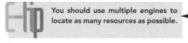

- HotMetal Pro
- Microsoft FrontPage

Other programs have multiple uses and have limited web-authoring capabilities, such as

- Corel NetPerfect
- Lotus FastSite
- Microsoft Publisher
- Microsoft Word

What Tools Are out There?

Establish an Internet connection, open your browser, then open your favorite search engine. You can use any search engine to locate web-authoring tools. Figures 5.3 and 5.4 show results of searches using two different search engines. Notice that both search engines returned different results.

Figures 5.5 and 5.6 display some of the additional resources you can find using the Web. You may find coverage choppy and inconsistent from one site to another. By visiting a variety of sites, you'll increase your knowledge tremendously and be able to form your own opinions.

E-tip

You should use multiple engines to locate as many resources as possible.

E-Tip

When you start to get frustrated or need assistance on the Web, look for an *E-Tip*. These boxes provide additional help when doing research or work on the Internet.

must deliver the product or service and may incur charges such as shipping. Until you are paid, you will be bearing these costs.

Customers can be fickle when it comes to price. Charge too much and they may think you're trying to take advantage. Charge too little and they may suspect the quality. Your price should be just right: low enough to entice, reasonable for its quality, and enabling you to cover your expenses and make a profit. You can always use short-term price promotions such as sales, coupons, and other incentives to tempt customers.

Look down the line at the evolution of the market when determining price strategies. Take into consideration all the costs associated with the marketing mix.

How Do I Promote My Business?

The way in which you promote the intentions of your business generally has a direct effect on sales. The levels of communication widely used include advertising, public relations, sales efforts, and reaching out to potential customers.

Regardless of the method of promotion, the goal is to entice the customer to buy your product or service. To achieve this goal, you may choose to expose potential customers to your business name whenever possible.

 Ideally, you want customers to think of you first. Your business should be at the top of a customer's mental list.

There are three basic objectives of promotion: to inform, persuade, and remind. This means that your promotional strategy is not to advertise only when you have a sale, but to *inform* them about what you do and why your function is necessary. Once you have educated customers of the necessity of your product or service, you can *persuade* them that they stand to gain from your business. Constant *reminders* reinforce your existence to the customer.

How Will My Customers Buy from Me?

As an eBusiness, it is reasonable to expect that your customers will make purchases from you online. In most cases, they will probably buy products or services from you using your website, although you may also offer customers telephone access through a toll-free number.

EBusinesses that sell customized products often rely on sophisticated software that enables the customer to pick and choose options to create a specific, personalized product.

How Can I Calculate a Marketing Budget?

Most businesses want to get spectacular marketing results while spending as little as possible. Unfortunately, marketing is expensive, and its results are not immediately realized. Some marketing effects are realized over long periods of time and are difficult to measure precisely.

There are four methods of determining the size of your marketing budget. These methods are also discussed in the website shown in Figure 3.15.

- Create a budget based on an agreed upon percentage of previous or projected sales. While this method creates a realistic budget for current production, it does not account for shifts in the marketplace; it assumes a direct relationship between marketing expenditures and sales results.

WEB ALERT!

Find links that help you learn more about enabler software at the website for this book.

Web Alert

Whenever there is information on the Web that can provide additional instruction or assistance, you will find a *Web Alert!* with a listing of the applicable web address(s) for you to check out.

Business Gift

If you are not familiar with various aspects of how a business is started or what tools and procedures are needed, you can find explanations and advice summaries for these within the *Business Gift*.

BUSINESS Gift

BUSINESS LAW

You probably wouldn't dream of starting a business without consulting an accountant, but do you need a lawyer? In addition to helping you choose and set up your corporate structure (sole proprietorship, partnership, or corporation), an attorney can provide you with business advice and prevent unforeseen liabilities. If your business requires patents or needs protection due to the use of intellectual property, your attorney should either be able to help you or provide a referral.

Your attorney should be able to help with all aspects of your business, including creating a structure that minimizes your personal liability in the event the business fails. A lawyer can also help you with product liability, warrantees, and advertising decisions and should minimize you and your business exposure to damages.

how to be an effective leader and good manager. Why, then, do so many people hate their bosses? With the number of seminars and self-help books available, shouldn't we have taught everyone how to be an effective leader by now?

Often the problem is not in the training but in the trainees. You not only have to want to be an effective leader, but you must see your flaws and, most important, be willing and able to make corrections.

What Makes a Leader Effective?

What qualities do you admire in a leader? The hands-down guru of management training is Stephen Covey, whose website is shown in Figure 8.4. Think of a leader, either well known or obscure, and make a list of what you feel makes this person great. In addition to being honest, supportive, and fair-minded, effective leaders have the ability to inspire, to enlist others in a shared vision, and to develop a collaborative effort.

The role of leadership within a company cannot be understated. As simple as the title implies, a *leader* shows others the way. Leadership can be as complex as outlining a sophisticated business plan, complete with time lines and financial forecasts, and as simple as keeping formality to a minimum and calling co-workers by their first names. The leader sets the tone and is the ultimate role model for the organization. If the leader isn't devoted to the company, the employees won't be.

Whether the destination is a hike in the woods or bringing a new product to market, the leader gets us there. The leader's abilities determine just how pleasurable and enriching that trip will be. A truly effective leader shares his or her vision with the group and makes that vision a reality. Sometimes the leader is forced to make unpopular decisions, such as firing team members.

An effective leader does not look for yes-men who only agree. Challenge and dissent make team members think, bringing new ideas and new methods to light. An effective leader is not afraid to challenge the status quo and is not leery of ideas that come from others. The changing landscape of the leadership market can be seen in Figure 8.5.

THE EDGE
Some of the best leadership tips are found not in how-to guides but in the biographies of effective leaders.

THE EDGE
Bureaucracy and routines are surefire ways of inhibiting creativity. They discourage risk taking, an essential element in the creative process.

Brief Contents

CHAPTER 1 Getting Started on the Web 2

CHAPTER 2 Creating a Business Plan 26

CHAPTER 3 Developing a Marketing Plan 46

CHAPTER 4 Designing a Web Page 66

CHAPTER 5 Creating a Website 86

CHAPTER 6 Enhancing a Web Page 106

CHAPTER 7 Creating Advanced Web Pages 126

CHAPTER 8 Running an eBusiness 144

Index 160

Contents

CHAPTER 1

Getting Started on the Web.......... 2

How Are Business Goals and Needs Defined? 4
What Should I Consider?...................... 5
Why Have a Web Presence? 6
Making My Site Known? 6
What Is in a Web Page? 7
What Are Typical Web Page Components? 7
What Makes for Good Web Pages? 10
What Is a Hyperlink?....................... 10
How Do I Use a Hyperlink? 11
What Is a Browser? 13
How Do I Get a Browser? 13
How Do I Choose a Browser? 13
What Is a Portal?.......................... 15
How Do I Sign Up to Use a Portal? 16
How Do I Customize a Portal? 17
How Do I Find Information on the Web? 18
What Tools Can I Use to Find Information? 18
Are There Searching Rules? 19
What Is a Mail Client? 20
How Do I Stay in Touch? 20
How Do I Close a Web Page and End a Web Session?................................. 23
How Do I Close a Browser? 23
How Do I End a Session? 23
Checkpoint 24
Keys 24
Milestones 24
Your Turn 24

CHAPTER 2

Creating a Business Plan 26

Do I Need a Business Plan? 28
Who Will Read the Business Plan? 28
What Is in the Business Plan? 28
How Do I Start My Business Plan? 30
How Do I Describe My Business?........... 30
In What Industry Is the Business Competing? 30
What Is the Purpose of Your Business?......... 32
What Products or Services Will the Business Provide?................................ 33
Where Does the Business Fit in the Market? 34
What Will I Charge Customers? 34
How Is My Market Analyzed?.............. 34
Who Are My Customers? 34
What Is the Market? 35
Who Is the Competition? 35
What Are My Estimated Sales?.............. 35
How Is My Product/Service Produced? 36
How Is a Product or Service Developed?........ 36
How Is a Product or Service Produced?........ 37
How Much Will It Cost?.................... 37
What Are the Nonmanagerial Labor Requirements?........................... 37
What Other Financial Information Is Necessary? 38
What Are My Strategies? 38
How Will I Sell and Market My Products/Services? 38
How Will I Distribute My Products/Services?..... 39
How Will I Advertise and Promote My Products/Services? 39
What Staff Is Needed? 40

Who Is Managing the Business? 40
Who Owns the Business? 40
Who Is on the Board of Directors? 40
Who Are My Support Services? 41

What Are My Financial Considerations? 41
How Do I Assess the Risks? 41
What Is the Cash Flow Statement? 42
What Is the Balance Sheet? 42
What Is the Income Statement? 42
How Much Money Do I Need? 42

Checkpoint 43
Keys 43
Milestones 44
Your Turn 44

CHAPTER 3

Developing a Marketing Plan 46

Why Is a Marketing Plan Necessary? 48
How Is the Marketing Plan Used? 48

How Do I Start the Marketing Plan? 49

What Factors Influence My Business? 50
What Are the Demands and Trends? 52
Is My Business Affected by Groups and
Organizations? 52
Who Are My Competitors? 52
What Is My Corporate Climate? 54

Who Are My Target Customers? 54

**What Are the Advantages of My Product or
Service?** 55
Why Should I Bring Up Problem Areas? 55
What Is My Industry Position? 57

What Are My Marketing Tactics? 58
What Should I Consider When Developing
Marketing Tactics? 58
How Do I Develop Tactics? 60

How Can I Calculate a Marketing Budget? . . . 61
What Should I Do? 62

Why Will My Business Succeed? 63
How Do I Implement the Marketing Plan? 64

Checkpoint 65
Keys 65
Milestones 65
Your Turn 65

CHAPTER 4

Designing a Web Page 66

How Do I Design an Effective Web Page? 68
How Do I Format Text? 69
What Should I Know about Graphic Design? . . . 72
How Can I Use Color? 75
How Should I Design a Form? 78
What Elements Can I Include in a Form? 78

**How Can I Create a Website for My
Business?** 80
How Can I Create a Website Using FrontPage? . . . 80
How Can I Create a Website Using Publisher? . . . 81

Where Can I Find Web Design Resources? 81

**What Should I Consider for Special-Needs
Audiences?** 82
What Special Needs Exist? 82

Checkpoint 84
Keys 84
Milestones 84
Your Turn 84

CHAPTER 5

Creating a Website 86

How Do I Plan a Website? 88
How Does a Web Page Differ from a Website? . . . 88
What Should I Be Thinking as I'm Planning My
Website? 88

How Can I Find Web-Authoring Tools? 88
What Tools Are out There? 89

What Is HTML? 92
What Does HTML Look Like? 92

How Is a Website Created? 93
How Can I Modify a Web Page? 96
How Do I Add a List to a Page? 98
How Can I Add a Hover Button? 99
How Can I Create a Navigation Bar? 102

Checkpoint 104
Keys 104
Milestones 104
Your Turn 105

CHAPTER 6

Enhancing a Web Page 106

What Is a Graphic Image? 108
   Which Format Should I Use? 108
   Are There Other Considerations? 109
Where Can I Get Images? 110
   What Kind of Image Topics Are Available? 110
How Can I Insert an Image? 110
How Is a Hyperlink Inserted? 114
How Are Multimedia Files Used? 116
   What Kind of Sites Are Available? 117
What Is a Form? 119
   Where Can I Find Forms? 119
   How Should a Form Be Designed? 119
How Is a Form Created? 120
How Can I Modify a Form? 121
Checkpoint 124
Keys 125
Milestones 125
Your Turn 125

CHAPTER 7

Creating Advanced Web Pages 126

Why Should I Use a Table? 128
How Is a Table Created? 128
How Can I Format a Table? 130
How Can I Use Colors and Borders? 132
How Can I Control Table Elements? 134

What Are Frames? 135
   How Can I Use Frames? 135
   Are There Frame Design Considerations? 135
How Can I Build Framed Pages? 137
How Can I Include Links in My Site? 140
Checkpoint 142
Keys 142
Milestones 142
Your Turn 142

CHAPTER 8

Running an eBusiness 144

How Much Accounting Should I Know? 146
   Are There Different Kinds of Accounting? 146
   What Are Basic Accounting Concepts? 147
   What Happens in Accounting? 147
   What Financial Statements Are Necessary? 148
What Management Techniques Are
Helpful? 148
   What Makes a Leader Effective? 149
How Can I Work from a Distance? 151
   How Can I Telecommute Effectively? 151
How Can I Get Help? 155
Checkpoint 157
Keys 157
Milestones 157
Your Turn 158

Index 160

Building an eBusiness

From the Ground Up

CHAPTER 1

Ramping Up

How Do You Get Started?

For quite a while, Cari dreamed of having her own business. In the last year, she had developed an idea for a web-based business that she could operate from her home. She mentioned the idea to friends and family members, and they were all supportive and encouraging.

What held Cari back more than anything was her lack of finely tuned web and business skills and, of course, her need for capital. She watched her children navigate the Web with snap and polish and was more than a little intimidated by their enthusiasm. She purchased several books, but each one made assumptions of knowledge that she lacked. If she could just nail down the basics, she might be able to fine-tune her business idea and be that much closer to making her dream come true.

Getting Started on the Web

FIGURE 1.1
Realizing Dreams

CHAPTER OUTLINE

How Are Business Goals and Needs Defined?

Why Have a Web Presence?

What Is in a Web Page?

What Is a Hyperlink?

What Is a Browser?

What Is a Portal?

How Do I Find Information on the Web?

What Is a Mail Client?

How Do I Close a Web Page and End a Web Session?

How Are Business Goals and Needs Defined?

If you are contemplating a new business that will utilize the Web, you're probably asking yourself a lot of questions. You cannot begin such an important endeavor without defining some key elements. You may have heard the terms eCommerce and eBusiness used in discussions about web-based businesses. These terms are often used interchangeably, but they do have different meanings. All companies conducting business over the Internet are involved in **eCommerce.** Each individual company conducting business over the Internet is an **eBusiness.**

E-tip Traditional companies in which customers are engaged in a building or storefront are referred to as **bricks-and-mortar businesses.**

In what field or category does your business fit? Will you sell a product or provide a service? For example, a company that sells computer equipment is a **product business** because it sells physical items to its customers. Before they are sold, inventory or finished products can be warehoused and may or may not be customized for a client. A company that troubleshoots computers is a **service business** because its clients pay for knowledge and expertise. While a service business may produce a tangible product, it is often created specifically for a client and may be highly customized.

How interactive does your website have to be in order to conduct your business? Some businesses, such as the one shown in Figure 1.2, use a website merely to introduce the company or event; they ask you to send an e-mail or call directly to establish a relationship. They may offer helpful information or related links, but in order to do business with them, you'll have to write, call, or visit a physical

FIGURE 1.2

Noninteractive
Website

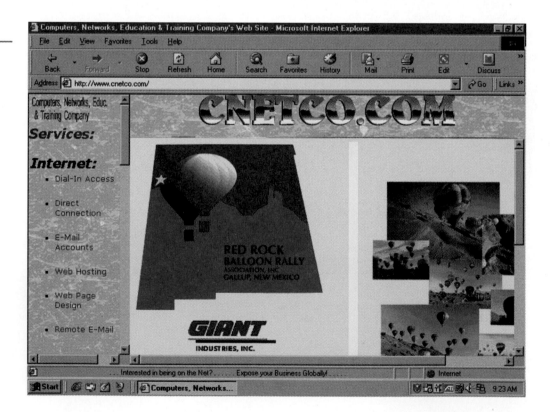

location. Other websites, such as the one shown in Figure 1.3, are highly interactive, enabling a customer to design a product and place an order without ever speaking to a real, live person. Table 1.1 contains examples of some product and service businesses.

What Should I Consider?

If your business sells a product, do you have suppliers lined up to satisfy your orders? How will you take orders? How will you deliver the product to your customers? If your business provides services, how will you interact with your clients? How will you transmit information from a customer to the actual service providers? What level of success are you striving for, and how hard are you willing to work to achieve these goals?

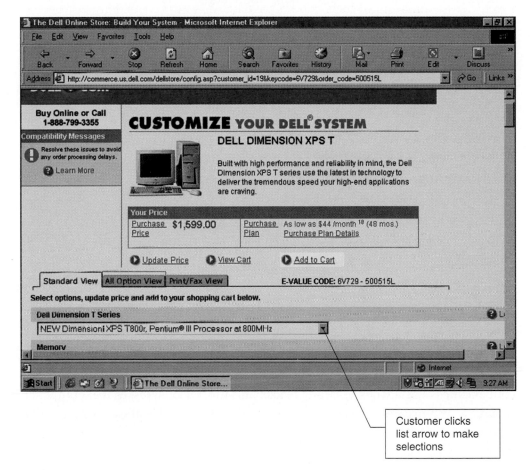

FIGURE 1.3

Interactive Website

Business	Type	Business	Type
Computer hardware	Product	Book vendor	Product
Architectural plans	Service	Astrology	Service
Plumbing supplies	Product	Web page design	Service

TABLE 1.1

Sample Product and Service Businesses

What Are My Future Concerns?

Some of these considerations may seem very advanced, but they are necessary if you are to come up with realistic goals. From these goals, you can establish just what your new eBusiness will need to make it a reality.

If your eBusiness creates products, it will need supplies to fulfill customer orders. You may have to consider the following:

- Why should a customer buy your product?
- Do you have any competition?
- Are your prices competitive?
- Will your business be conducted using an interactive website?
- How many suppliers are available?
- Will supplier cost influence which vendor you use?
- Is there a difference in quality among suppliers?
- Can the supplier deliver when promised?
- Will you make a profit based on the price you will be charging?
- Who will deliver the finished product?

Service organizations have some different considerations from those businesses that create products. You might want to think about the following:

- Why should a customer use your services?
- Do you have any competition?
- Are your prices competitive?
- How many services will you offer?
- Will you bill a flat fee for services, or charge for time and materials?
- If you are charging a flat fee, can you make a profit based on your expenses?
- Can you conduct business using only your website?
- Is it necessary to meet your clients in order to conduct business?

Why Have a Web Presence?

A business may want a web presence for many reasons. A **web presence** means your business has a website. Many bricks-and-mortar businesses feel compelled to have a web presence just to stay competitive. A pure eBusiness—one with no physical storefront—*must* have a web presence, since it is the only method of interacting with the public.

Making My Site Known

There are thousands of pages on the Internet, but that doesn't mean you can find them all when you need them. Have you ever wondered how it is that sites are listed when you do a search with your favorite search engine? Figure 1.4 shows the results of a search for "spaghetti sauce." Your Aunt Grace may produce and sell a fabulous sauce. She may even have a great website, but it's not great if no one can find and view the site. The only way a website can be found by search engines is to make sure it is registered.

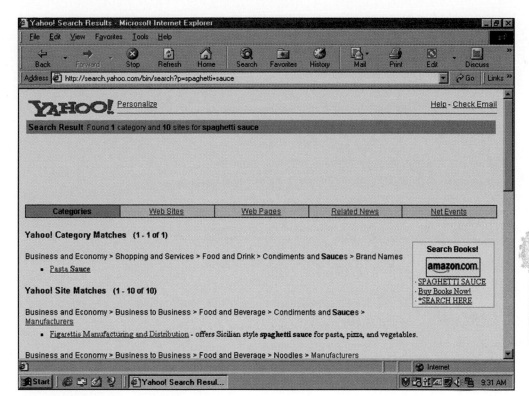

FIGURE 1.4

Search Results

WEB ALERT!

Use key words such as "website registration" in your favorite search engine to locate sites that help develop a web presence.

Source: Reproduced with permission of Yahoo! Inc. ©2000 by Yahoo! Inc. Yahoo! and the Yahoo! logo are trademarks of Yahoo! Inc.

How Do I Register My Site?

Registering your website can be as easy as locating a registration site, like the ones shown in Figures 1.5 and 1.6 and following the instructions for registration. Most of these services offer several tiers of registration and, given the exposure they provide, are well worth their fees.

What Is in a Web Page?

Most websites are the result of careful planning. Most eBusinesses use a series of pages that the reader can easily access from the initial page. The initial page in a website, called the **home page,** introduces the business and establishes a visual theme that will be carried over to each subsequent page. The similar appearance of each page provides continuity to the site and lets the reader know what to expect and where to find information. While there are no hard-and-fast rules for what you'll find in web pages, there are some components that you will see with increasing frequency.

What Are Typical Web Page Components?

Most companies—whether they are strictly eBusinesses or bricks-and-mortar—have established an identity with an easily recognizable logo. A **logo** is traditionally any combination of a color, shape, or text containing the company name or slogan. When you see a logo, such as the Coca-Cola banner or the Nike swoosh, you automatically think of that company. Think of a logo as a company's national flag.

THE EDGE

Begin the registration process early in your website design. You want potential customers to find your site as soon as it is online.

FIGURE 1.5

Web Site Garage Page

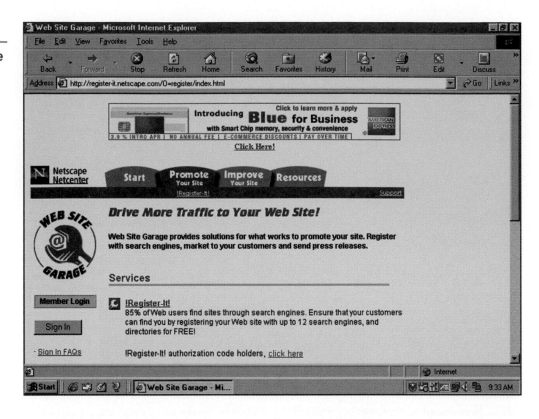

FIGURE 1.6

SubmitIt! Page

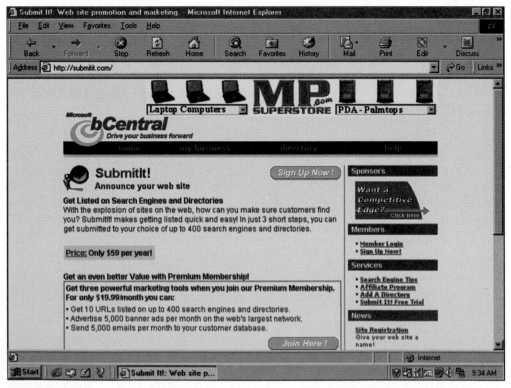

Source: Screen shot reprinted by permission from Microsoft Corporation.

INTERNET IDENTITY

On the Web, no one knows the size of your business. You might have the largest warehouse, stocked to the rafters with impressive merchandise, or you might be a small mom-and-pop operation with no warehouse at all. Because the Web gives eBusinesses a certain amount of anonymity, what separates you from the big boys is customer service, not size. All things being equal, you may be able to outclass larger businesses because you provide more and better customer service.

It is ironic that in eCommerce—which is sometimes considered more *impersonal* than traditional bricks-and-mortar businesses—you can create a *more personal* atmosphere with top-notch customer service.

FIGURE 1.7

McGraw-Hill Home Page

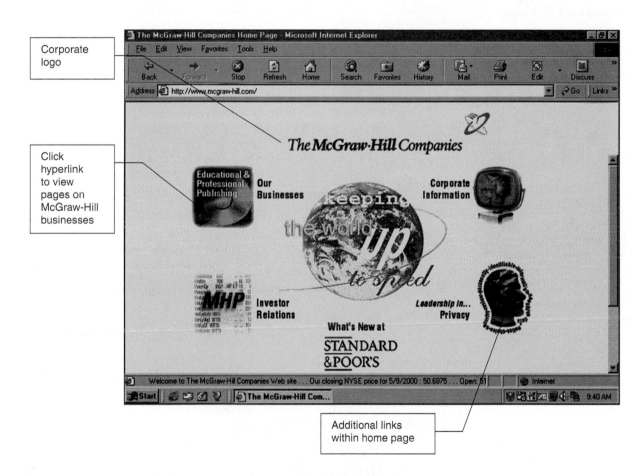

Figure 1.7 shows the home page for The McGraw-Hill Companies. Notice the logo in the upper-right corner of the page? This logo is also seen in Figure 1.8, providing continuity between the pages.

Most websites feature the corporate logo on every page as a way of establishing a constant theme. Some businesses may have separate, distinct logos for divisions within their company, as seen in Figure 1.9.

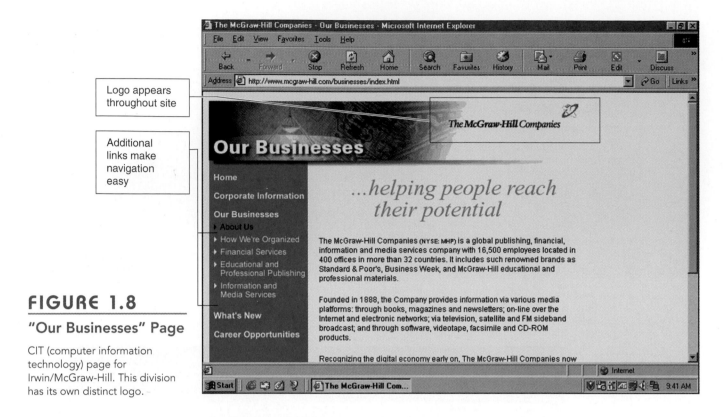

Logo appears throughout site

Additional links make navigation easy

FIGURE 1.8

"Our Businesses" Page

CIT (computer information technology) page for Irwin/McGraw-Hill. This division has its own distinct logo.

Take Note

When you visit other websites, be aware of how certain elements affect you. Do you like particular colors or elements? Make a mental note of those features you'd like to incorporate into your own site. Be conscious of features you find irritating and want to avoid using.

What Makes for Good Web Pages?

It's not always that easy to describe what you like, but it's generally very easy to determine what you don't like. As you look through various pages, look not only at page content but also at design. Remember that you don't have to fit all your business information on a single page; spread the information out to many pages. For example, you might want a separate page to talk about your corporate vision, one for items you carry or services you provide, and one for any warranties that are available.

Several design principles found within good websites are:

- Readability, with an uncluttered look.
- Soothing, easy-to-read colors that don't distract from their content.
- Understandable wording that doesn't intimidate your readers.
- Navigation that enables your readers to easily get to pages within your site.
- Graphics that are small enough to easily download and enhance the site.
- Multimedia that adds value to the site.

What Is a Hyperlink?

One of the features that makes the Internet more than just a bunch of pretty pages is that you can jump from one page to another. This is accomplished through careful and deliberate planning of the site designer. Each time you click a link, or **hyperlink,** you are automatically taken to a different web page. Each hyperlink is an instruction to a new website, and this instruction contains an Internet address called a **URL (Uniform Resource Locator).** The default setting in many

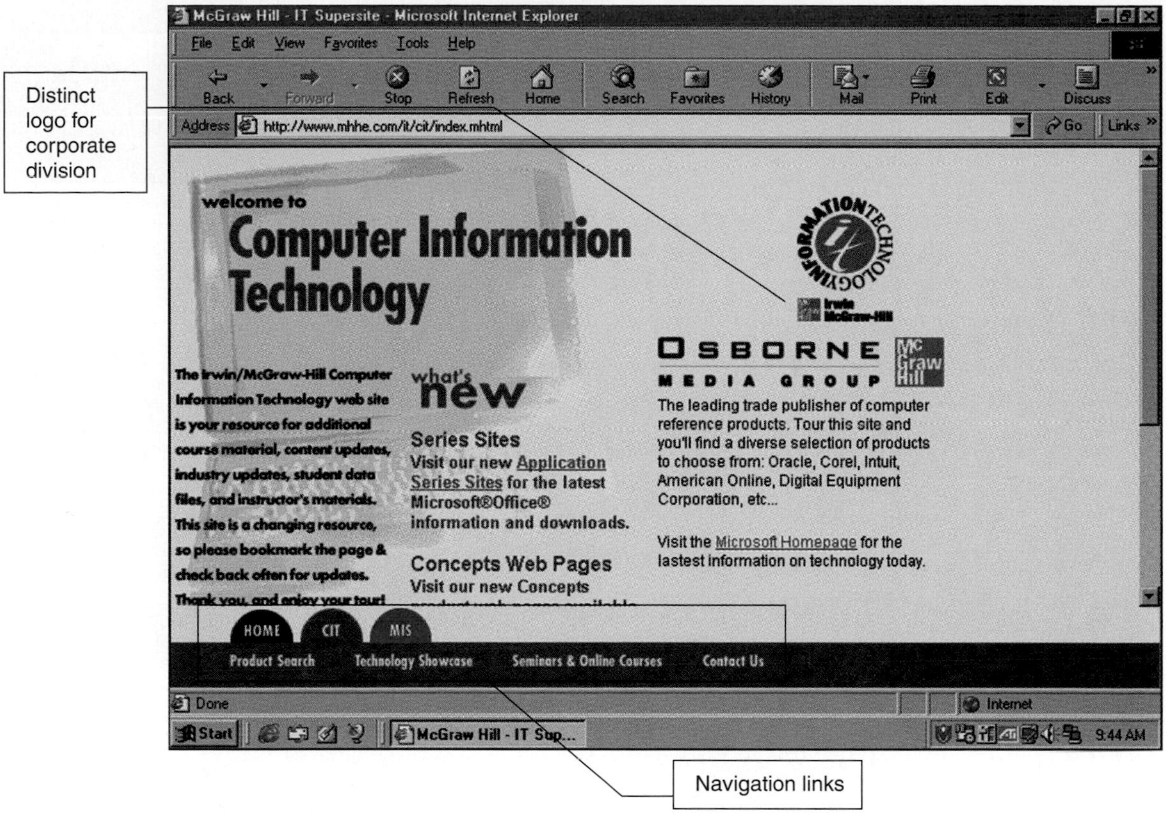
Distinct logo for corporate division
McGraw Hill - IT Supersite - Microsoft Internet Explorer
File Edit View Favorites Tools Help
Back Forward Stop Refresh Home Search Favorites History Mail Print Edit Discuss
Address http://www.mhhe.com/it/cit/index.mhtml
Go Links
welcome to
Computer Information Technology
The Irwin/McGraw-Hill Computer Information Technology web site is your resource for additional course material, content updates, industry updates, student data files, and instructor's materials. This site is a changing resource, so please bookmark the page & check back often for updates.
what's new
Series Sites
Visit our new Application Series Sites for the latest Microsoft®Office® information and downloads.
Concepts Web Pages
Visit our new Concepts
INFORMATION TECHNOLOGY
Irwin McGraw-Hill
OSBORNE MEDIA GROUP
Mc Graw Hill
The leading trade publisher of computer reference products. Tour this site and you'll find a diverse selection of products to choose from: Oracle, Corel, Intuit, American Online, Digital Equipment Corporation, etc...
Visit the Microsoft Homepage for the lastest information on technology today.
HOME CIT MIS
Product Search Technology Showcase Seminars & Online Courses Contact Us
Done
Internet
Start
McGraw Hill - IT Sup...
9:44 AM
Navigation links

FIGURE 1.9

CIT Page

computers shows text containing a hyperlink in blue and underlined. In addition to text, a hyperlink can also be a graphic image. There are a variety of hyperlinks shown in Figure 1.10. When you click the link click here you are automatically taken to a new location.

Web pages are written in a language called **HTML (HyperText Markup Language),** which defines how text and images appear on the Web using a series of tags. The tagging system makes it possible for pages written on one type of computer to be understood and displayed by different types of computers.

E-tip: When you position the mouse pointer over a hyperlink, the pointer changes from ↖ to ☝.

How Do I Use a Hyperlink?

You can use a hyperlink by clicking on either the linked text click here or by clicking a linked graphic image.

E-tip: Single-click or double-click? You only need to single-click a hyperlink to make it active.

Steps

1. Establish an Internet connection, if necessary.
2. Open your browser, and then click the URL text box.
3. Type **www.bedbathandbeyond.com,** then press **Enter.**
4. Point to **Bedding,** point to **Sheets,** then click **Prints.** Compare your screen to Figure 1.11.
5. Close your browser.
6. Close your Internet connection, if necessary.

FIGURE 1.10

Hyperlinks in Web
Page

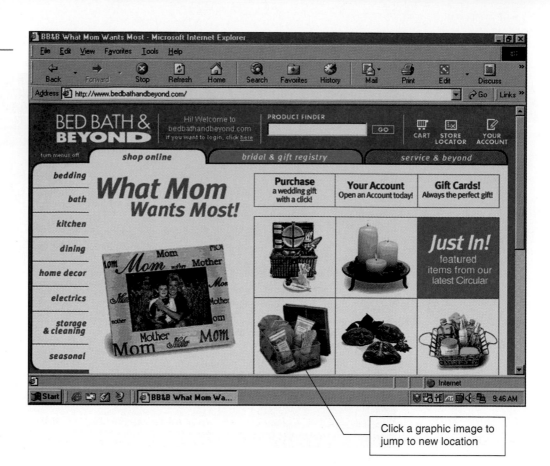

Click a graphic image to
jump to new location

FIGURE 1.11

Result of Using
Hyperlink

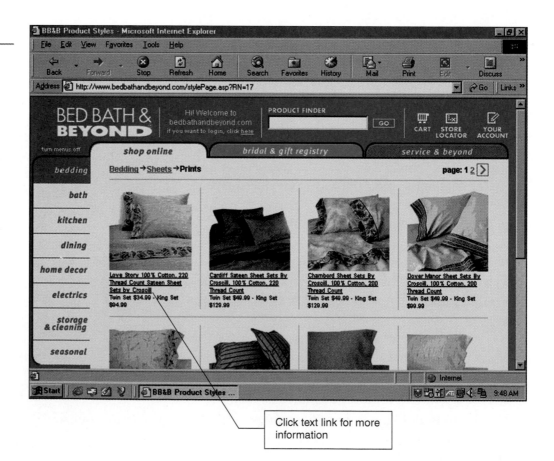

Click text link for more
information

What Is a Browser?

To use the World Wide Web, we use a browser. A **browser** is a software program that lets you access the content of websites. Each time you open your browser, it automatically displays a page, called your **home page.** Currently available browsers display colorful pages and hyperlinks, as well as frames and multimedia files, including video clips and sounds.

In addition to multimedia—which just about all browsers can display—some pages contain applets. An **applet** is a miniature program designed to run either when the page is opened or when an image is clicked. Applets are generally written in Java or ActiveX.

Take Note

Your browser's ability to run Java or ActiveX will affect the appearance of a web page.

How Do I Get a Browser?

For many computer users, the decision to use a browser may be made for them. Many computer resellers, such as Gateway and Dell, have agreements with vendors to install their browsers on new machines or include their software with the units.

How Do I Choose a Browser?

The browser market is very competitive. Although there are other browsers, the two chief rivals are Microsoft Internet Explorer and Netscape Navigator. Figure 1.12 shows a web page in Internet Explorer; Figure 1.13 shows the same page in Netscape Navigator. While strikingly similar, there are subtle differences in color.

FIGURE 1.12

Internet Explorer Browser

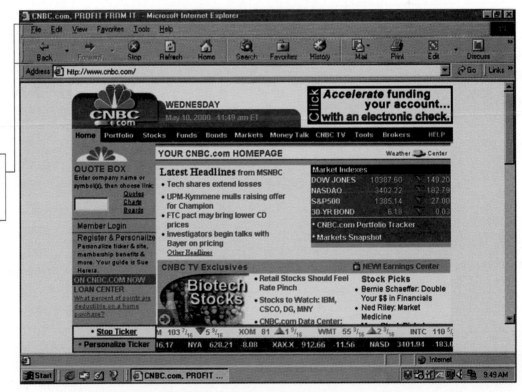

Unique menu and toolbar buttons

FIGURE 1.13

Netscape Navigator
Browser

Different options for many of the same functions

Additional features in floating palette

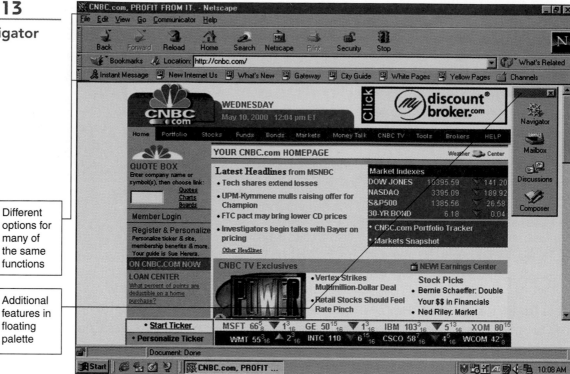

BUSINESS *Gift*

BOOKMARKING WEB SITES

Have you ever found a perfect site, only to be unable to find it again? Most browsers let you build a list of favorite sites. These lists, called **favorites** or **bookmarks,** let you create manageable lists of sites that you can organize in meaningful categories.

In Internet Explorer, shown in Figure 1.14, you can add a site to your favorites list by going to the site, clicking Favorites on the menu bar, then clicking Add to Favorites. In Netscape Navigator, you can click the Bookmarks button, then click Add Bookmark, as shown in Figure 1.15. Regardless of which browser you use, creating bookmarks or favorites mean you can always return to a great site.

Like other programs, most browsers let you make selections using menu command or toolbar buttons.

Web pages can differ when displayed in different browsers. Technological innovations may make it necessary to update your browser software. If your browser is current, you'll be able to take advantage of new web page effects. As browser software becomes more sophisticated, browsers seem to converge, with each one having the same capabilities. Some users base browser preference on past performance and comfort

As you experiment with different browsers, you may notice a variation between screen loading times.

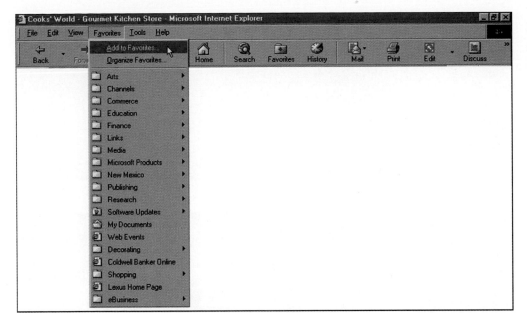

FIGURE 1.14

Adding a Favorite in Internet Explorer

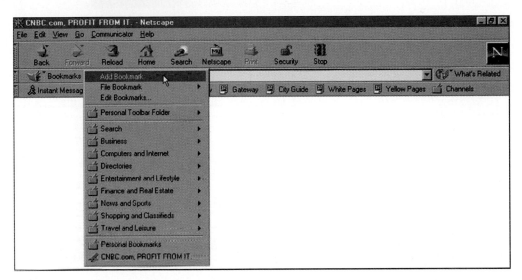

FIGURE 1.15

Creating a Bookmark in Netscape Navigator

level. You may be comfortable with Internet Explorer and like its look and feel. Or maybe you've been using Netscape Navigator and prefer that browser.

What Is a Portal?

As a user of the Internet, you constantly want more and more information. With increased familiarity, you'll find a site that lets you get a lot of information in a single page. A site that gives you a lot of information about various topics and lets you customize that page is called a **portal.** Table 1.2 lists some portal sites. Many portals give you the options of seeing local weather and news, national and international news, stock prices, and news on a variety of subjects. Portal sites can crop up in unusual places, such as financial services, search engines, and regional television stations. Check your local newspaper or radio station to see if its site is a portal. Figure 1.16 contains a table that compares features in various portals.

Once you find a portal that meets your needs, you can always turn that site into your home page.

TABLE 1.2

Commonly Available Portals

Owner/Sponsor	URL
Yahoo	http://www.yahoo.com
Netscape	http://www.netscape.com
Microsoft	http://home.microsoft.com
Snap	http://www.snap.com
Go Network	http://www.go.com
CNBC	http://www.cnbc.com

FIGURE 1.16

Comparison of Portals

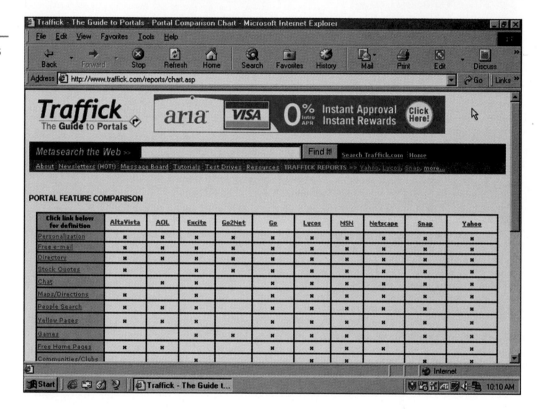

How Do I Sign Up to Use a Portal?

To use the features within a portal, most require that you sign in or register with the site. In most cases, this registration is free, but most sites require that you answer some demographic information.

Steps

1. Establish an Internet connection, if necessary, open your browser, then click the URL text box.
2. Type **www.go2net.com,** then press **Enter.**
3. Click the **Customize** hyperlink.
4. Click the **Sign up now!** hyperlink.
5. Click the **Username** text box, then type a name you want to use to log in to the site.
6. Click the **Password** text box, then type a name you can remember as a password.

7. Click the **Confirm Password** text box, then retype your password.

8. Fill in the remaining required fields, then click **Register Me.**

9. Close your browser, then close your Internet connection, if necessary.

How Do I Customize a Portal?

Most portals have controls within them that make it easy for you to customize. Most portals let you display specific stocks, local weather, and other information and arrange the layout of items on the page.

Steps

1. Establish an Internet connection, if necessary, open your browser, then click the URL text box.

2. Type **www.go2net.com,** then press **Enter.**

3. Click the **Customize this page** hyperlink, the **Today Page Layout** appears, as shown in Figure 1.17.

4. Click the **Stocks** down arrow.

5. Click **Return to Main Page.**

6. Compare your page to Figure 1.18.

7. Close your browser.

8. Close your Internet connection, if necessary.

FIGURE 1.17

Customizing a Portal's Layout

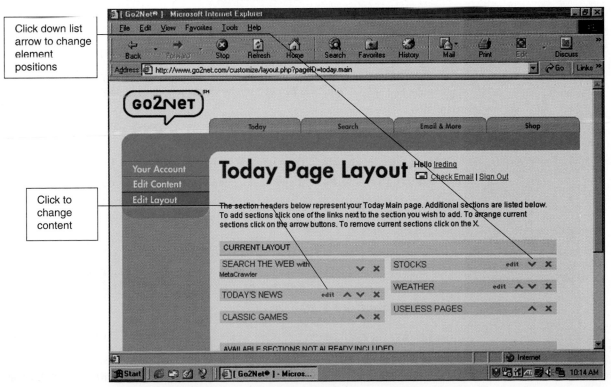

Source: Used by permission of Go2net, Inc. All rights reserved.

FIGURE 1.18

Customized Portal

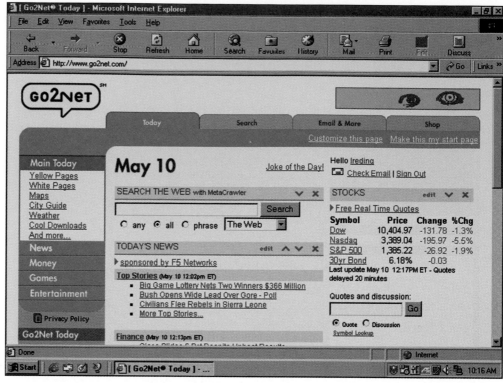

How Do I Find Information on the Web?

E-tip

It's important that you maintain your focus while conducting your search, or you can easily become sidetracked.

WEB ALERT!

Use key words such as "web searches" in your favorite search engine to locate search tools.

THE EDGE

Use a directory when looking for information in clearly defined categories, such as airlines or tires.

THE EDGE

Use a search engine when looking for information not in clearly defined categories.

Sometimes the amount of information available on the Internet seems unlimited. There is so much information on topics of great interest to you that it's easy to get overwhelmed and sidetracked. In order to separate what you want from what you don't want, you can use a search service. A **search service** is a software device that helps you locate information on the Web.

What Tools Can I Use to Find Information?

There are two main classifications of search services on the Internet: directories and search engines. Most web users combine these two categories together and (incorrectly) refer to any site that helps you locate information as a search engine.

What Is a Directory?

A **directory** is a search service that classifies websites into a hierarchical subject-based structure. Such a service may define sites using descriptive categories such as Media, Entertainment, and Travel. Figure 1.19 shows the Yahoo site, one of the best known directory search services.

What Is a Search Engine?

A **search engine** is a search service that indexes keywords within some or all documents in websites. **Keywords** are found within a document and have contextual

FIGURE 1.19

Yahoo Directory Site

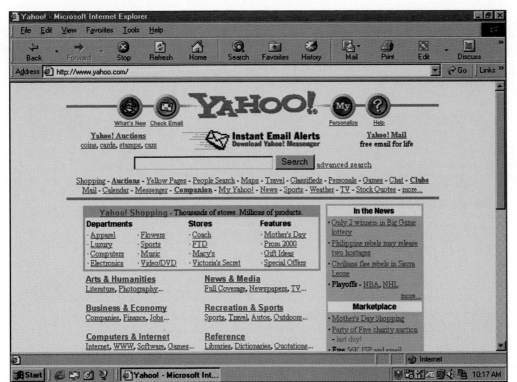

Source: Source: Reproduced with permission of Yahoo! Inc. ©2000 by Yahoo! Inc. Yahoo! and the Yahoo! logo are trademarks of Yahoo! Inc.

meaning to that topic. A search engine matches your keywords with its index. Figure 1.20 shows the Excite site. Other examples of search engines are Infoseek and AltaVista.

Are There Searching Rules?

You can spend as much time searching for information as it takes to digest the information you find. Here are a few rules that can help solidify your results and minimize the amount of time spent in searches:

- Limit keywords to nouns and objects, not verbs, adjectives, or adverbs (example: house, home, apartment).
- Supply six to eight keywords. More words limit the results of the search to better matching documents (example: house, building, new, construction, mortgage).
- Use wildcards to match singular and plural words. The asterisk (*) wildcard tells a search engine to match the characters to the left of the asterisk and accept any characters to the right of the asterisk (example: build*, loan*).
- Match similar words or concepts using the OR operator (example: construction OR build*).
- Find exact matches of multiple keywords using AND (example: loan AND "first home").
- Find multiple word strings by combining keywords with quotation marks (example: "real estate").

FIGURE 1.20

Excite Search Engine

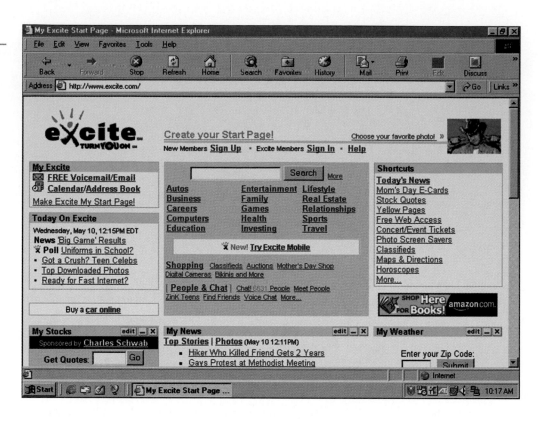

What Is a Mail Client?

As the operator of an e-business, staying in touch with your customers is key. How can you do this? By utilizing the environment in which you're conducting your business. E-mail is the most popular and important means of staying in touch with business and personal contacts. The software you use to receive, send, and organize your e-mail is called a **mail client.** Often, this software is included in the purchase price of a new computer and is already installed. Some commonly available mail clients are Microsoft Outlook or Lotus Notes. Mail clients are also typically bundled with office suite programs, such as Microsoft Office.

> **E-tip**
>
> When e-mail arrives in your account, it stays on your Internet Service Provider (ISP) server until it is delivered or you delete it.

How Do I Stay in Touch?

In any given day, a bricks-and-mortar entrepreneur will receive stacks of messages that take time and individual attention to return. The same is true of e-mail. Returning e-mail can become an onerous chore, but it is essential that these messages be answered in a timely fashion. Don't respond, and potential customers may do business with a competitor.

What Are My Options?

Most mail clients have similar features that permit common e-mail tasks. Table 1.3 lists some of the tasks that are useful in a business environment. The mail client in Figure 1.21 is Microsoft Outlook; the one in Figure 1.22 is Eudora Pro. Both programs allow you to organize messages in folders.

THE EDGE

Avoid sending large files of a personal nature in the business world. Not everyone may share your enthusiasm for a particular joke or graphic image.

Closed
envelope
means
unread
message

Bold text
indicates
unread
messages
in folder

Paper clip
indicates
an
attachment

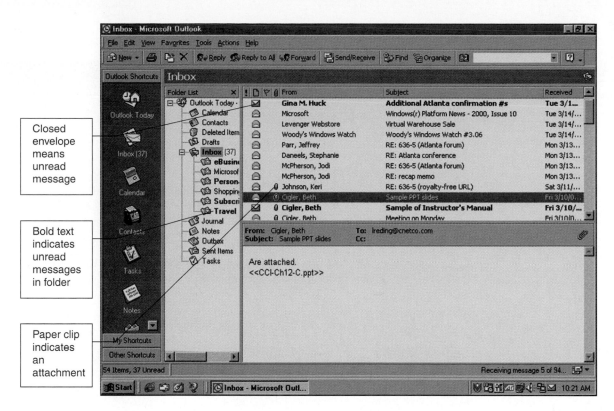

FIGURE 1.21

Microsoft Outlook Mail
Client

Organize
messages
in folders

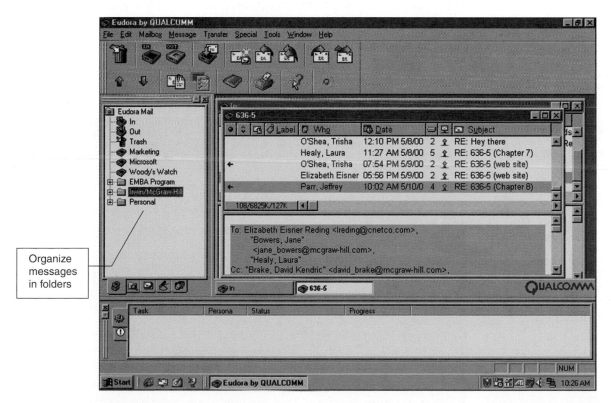

FIGURE 1.22

Eudora Pro Mail Client

TABLE 1.3

Common E-Mail Tasks

Feature/Task	When Do I Use This?
Send	To create a new message.
Reply	To respond to the author of a message.
Reply all	To respond to all recipients (and the author) of a message.
Forward	To send a message to another person.
Redirect	To send a message to another person and indicate the redirection.
Send attachment	To send an electronic file with a message.
Cc:	To send a copy of the message to a related party.
Bcc:	To send a hidden copy of the message to a related party. Bcc recipients remain anonymous to others.

BUSINESS Gift

MAKING A STATEMENT

Creating e-mail is not like writing the great American novel, but it is a means of expression that reflects your attitudes and your professionalism. You wouldn't mail a business memo that contained typos and coffee stains; you should be just as critical and sensitive when writing e-mail. Some people might argue that since e-mail, unlike mailed correspondence, can lurk in computer systems for an unlimited amount of time, it should be afforded even more respect than it typically receives.

It is reasonable to expect a response to a business e-mail within 24 hours. Anything more than that implies that either you don't check your e-mail or you don't consider it important. Figure 1.23 is a sample courtesy message you can send to your frequent business contacts. Such a message lets people know how long you'll be out of the office and the frequency with which you'll check your e-mail.

FIGURE 1.23

Courtesy E-Mail

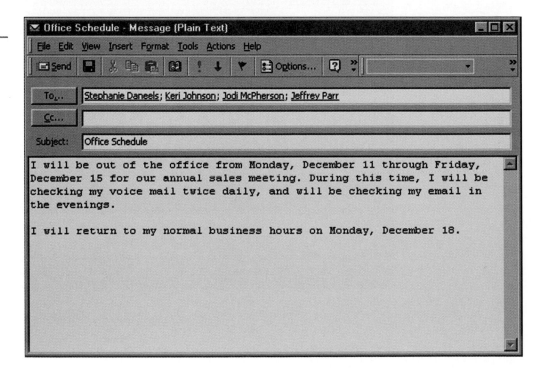

How Do I Close a Web Page and End a Web Session?

As with any program, you'll want to know how to end your session. The method you use to close a session depends on the service you have and how you make your connection. You can close your browser and end the session at any time.

How Do I Close a Browser?

Closing a web page is as simple as closing your browser. When you are finished with a particular session on the Web, you can close your browser by clicking the Close button. Figure 1.24 shows the features of a web page you can use to exit.

How Do I End a Session?

If you have an always-on service (such as T1, DSL, or cable modem), you do not have to disconnect from the Internet. If you use a dial-up service to access the Web, you will want to terminate your connection when you are finished with individual tasks. Figure 1.25 shows the dialog box that may appear when you close your browser.

Take Note

Dial-up account users should refrain from "camping out" (staying connected for long periods of time without any activity), as this may prevent others from accessing the service.

E-tip You can also terminate a dial-up session by double-clicking the connection icon in the system tray, then clicking the Disconnect button.

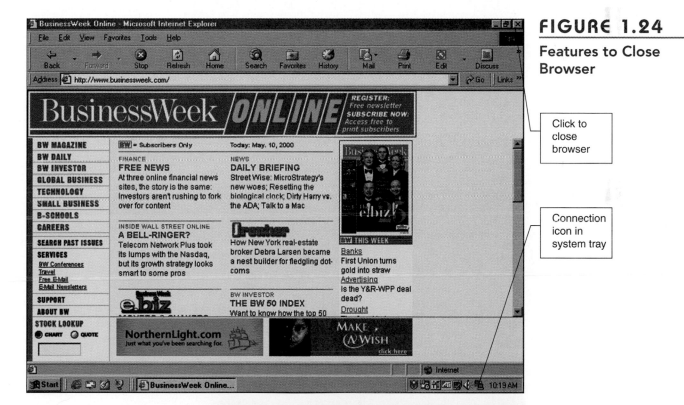

FIGURE 1.24

Features to Close Browser

Click to close browser

Connection icon in system tray

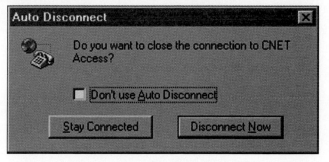

FIGURE 1.25

Auto Disconnect Dialog Box

Checkpoint

Before you can get an eBusiness off the ground, you need a basic understanding of Internet features. Starting a business means you will be asking yourself a barrage of questions. Will I be providing a service or product? Is my pricing fair and competitive? Can I make a profit? Can I make a fortune?

Once your goals and needs are firm, start thinking about how you would like your company website to look. What links must you provide? What links would your customers like to see? To provide the best for your customers, you must anticipate their needs and know what will please them.

Keys

eCommerce	hyperlink	favorites
eBusiness	URL (Uniform Resource	bookmarks
product business	Locator)	portal
service business	HTML (HyperText Markup	search service
bricks-and-mortar business	Language)	directory
web presence	browser	search engine
home page	home page	keywords
logo	applet	mail client

Milestones

Complete the following statements:

1. An online office supplies vendor is an example of a _____ business.
2. The first page that appears when your browser opens is the _____ page.
3. All companies doing business on the Internet are involved in _____.
4. A customizable website that can be used as a home page is called a _____.
5. A search service that uses broad categories to define a business is called a _____.

Complete the following exercises:

1. Find a portal website, then register and customize the page using your own preferences.
2. Create at least five bookmarks or favorites of sites you visit frequently.

Your Turn

It's time to turn the table on yourself. As an eBusiness customer, what are your expectations from an eBusiness that provides a product? What are your expectations from an eBusiness that provides a service? How can you incorporate your own expectations to provide better customer service to your customers?

CHAPTER 2

Planning

Why Write a Business Plan?

Since she was a child, Kim has always expressed herself through her jewelry creations. Given the eCommerce climate, she feels the timing is right to combine her artistic talents with her business skills. Family and friends love her creations, and she thinks there is a market for her jewelry. Perhaps she can attract a wider range of clients if she starts an eBusiness.

Kim also knows that she needs more than a great idea to make her eBusiness a success. She needs money and support. People at her local community college encouraged her to write a business plan. Kim wants to use the business plan to raise funds, but she also knows that writing the plan will help her solidify her business goals and help her formulate strategies.

Creating a Business Plan

CHAPTER OUTLINE

Do I Need a Business Plan?

How Do I Start My Business Plan?

How Do I Describe My Business?

How Is My Market Analyzed?

How Is My Product/Service Produced?

What Are My Strategies?

What Staff Is Needed?

What Are My Financial Considerations?

FIGURE 2.1
Planning

Do I Need a Business Plan?

You're probably asking yourself why you should write a business plan. If you're in the position of most start-ups, you're probably doing everything, and here's one more responsibility for which you don't have time. For most people, the thought of writing such a document is daunting, to say the least.

If the point of the business plan were to practice your writing skills, you'd be right to balk at taking this on. But the business plan is much more. If you need outside funding, the plan can be used to assure possible outside investors that your basic idea is sound and that it can succeed.

Of more importance than convincing others that your idea is sound, you should come away from writing your business plan *convincing yourself* that your business will succeed.

Who Will Read the Business Plan?

THE EDGE

As the head of your company, *you are the most important person* for whom the business plan is written.

The business plan is a road map for your success. Readers of your business plan run the gamut of people who can help you financially or emotionally. Some potential readers of your business plan might include

- Bankers—conventional money lenders.
- **Angels**—wealthy individuals who can provide you with seed money (usually under $1 million).
- **Venture capitalists**—generally firms that are willing to assume higher risk than conventional banks; they fund start-ups in return for equity in the business or stock.
- **Strategic partners**—businesses with which you may want to form alliances and work on joint projects.
- Potential employees—talented people you may want to attract and ultimately hire.
- Current employees—people already working with you who might be motivated by reading the plan.

What Is in the Business Plan?

There are many helpful print and web sources that show you how to write a successful business plan. Most sources list the necessary ingredients you should include. As you read these, you'll find several variations: some many contain more sections than others or may use different category names, but most suggest that a good business plan should include items in Table 2.1. Go on the Web and use your favorite search engine to find information on writing a business plan. Figure 2.2 shows a listing of websites that can help you get additional information about preparing a business plan.

E-Tip

As you look at various business plans, you may see these topics in different orders; some may be missing entirely. Sometimes the executive summary section is unnumbered. Let the specifics of your business dictate how the plan is structured.

THE EDGE

Readers of the executive summary are not only evaluating your business ideas, they are forming opinions about you. Make your delivery professional and convincing.

How Do I Start My Business Plan?

In addition to the cover page and table of contents, the first section in the business plan contains the executive summary. While it might seem odd to begin such an important document with a summary, the **executive summary** is most likely

Category	Contents
Introduction	The cover page
	Table of contents
	Executive summary
Business description	Provide an overview of your industry (current and future)
	Discuss your mission statement
	Define your products or services
	Describe your company's position in the market
	List your pricing strategies
Marketplace	Describe your target customer
	Define the size of the entire market and your target market
	List and describe your competitors
	Estimate your sales
Development and production	Describe the status of your product/service
	Describe the production process/service delivery
	Include a design and development budget
	Outline your (nonmanagement) labor requirements
	Include operating expenses, capital requirements, and cost of goods
Sales and marketing	Describe how you will find potential customers and how you will turn them into actual customers
	Define your distribution channels
	Outline your advertising and promotion campaign
Management	Outline who owns and controls the company
	Describe the management structure
	Outline members of the board of directors
	Determine your support services
Financial information	Assess potential risks
	Provide/analyze your cash flow statement
	Provide/analyze your balance sheet
	Provide/analyze your income statement
	Estimate your funding needs

TABLE 2.1

Necessary Business Plan Ingredients

the first thing a reader will look at, and it is usually the last section written. This summary is generally short—between one and three pages—and outlines the following items:

- Business concept.
- Financial features.
- Financial requirements.

THE EDGE
Use headers and footers to provide important information on each page of the plan.

FIGURE 2.2

Business Plan Search
Engine Results

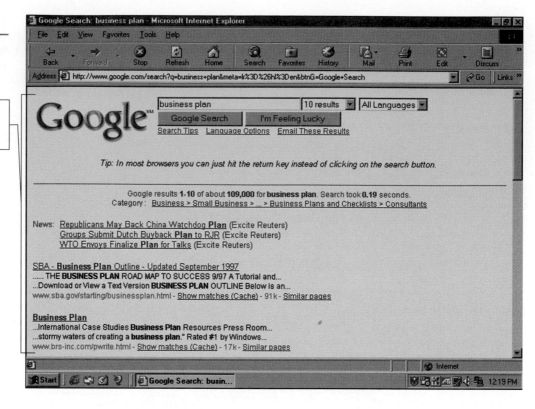

Your search
results may
differ

- Current state of the business and when it was formed.
- Principal owners and key participants.

In front of the executive summary is a cover page containing the name of the business and when the plan was prepared. What follows is a table of contents. Figure 2.3 shows a table of contents generated using Microsoft Word's table of contents feature. Using an automated table of contents feature requires a little planning *before* you begin writing, but it saves you time in the long run and produces a more professional-looking document.

To have Word generate a table of contents, create a blank page in the document, usually following the cover page, and define headings using the Style list box. Each heading level will appear indented in the table of contents. When you are ready to generate the table, position the pointer where you want the table to begin, click Insert on the menu bar, click Index and Tables, click the Table of Contents tab as shown in Figure 2.4, make any necessary settings changes, then click OK.

How Do I Describe My Business?

The section following the executive summary is called the **business description.** This is where you provide the reader with an in-depth description of the industry, your company, and the products or services being offered; where you fit in the marketplace; and how you plan to charge for your products or services.

In What Industry Is the Business Competing?

Regardless what your business does, it fits in some **industry,** or niche. And since you can't assume your reader knows the implications of the industry, it is up to you to provide a brief overview. Because no one wants to be in business for only

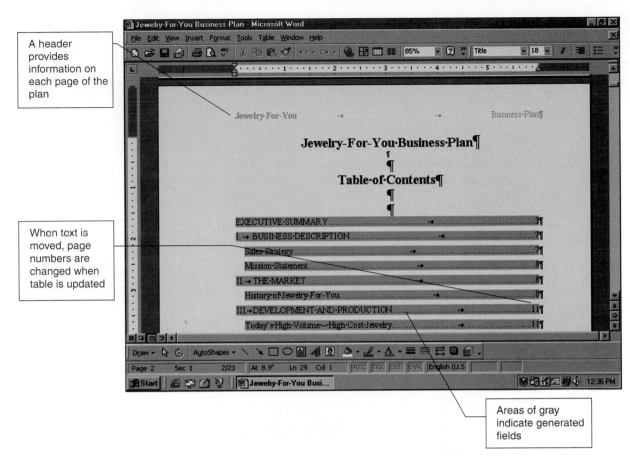

A header provides information on each page of the plan

When text is moved, page numbers are changed when table is updated

Areas of gray indicate generated fields

FIGURE 2.3

Table of Contents Generated in Microsoft Word

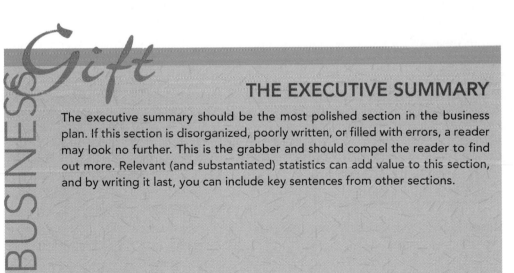

THE EXECUTIVE SUMMARY

The executive summary should be the most polished section in the business plan. If this section is disorganized, poorly written, or filled with errors, a reader may look no further. This is the grabber and should compel the reader to find out more. Relevant (and substantiated) statistics can add value to this section, and by writing it last, you can include key sentences from other sections.

a short time, you will want to emphasize that your entry into this market has an excellent long-term outlook and that there is growth potential for your business.

What Is the Industry Outlook?

Paint a realistic image of the industry. Is it a new and exciting field with limitless possibilities? Is it established, mature, and in place? Let your enthusiasm show; the reader should be jazzed by your description.

Take Note

If an article or report adds value to your plan, include it in an appendix.

FIGURE 2.4

Table of Contents Tab in Index and Tables Dialog Box

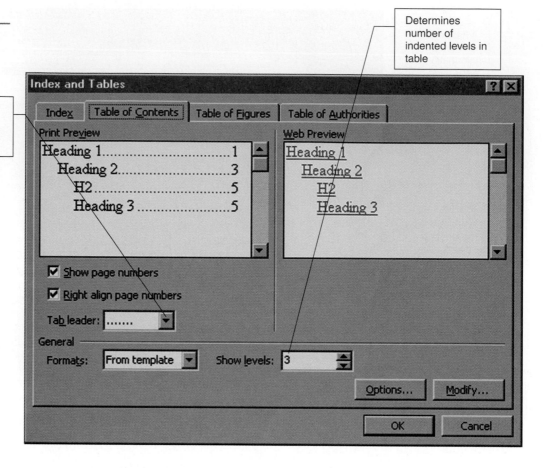

Statements about the industry's health should answer any questions the reader might have. If, for example, you say there is great growth potential over the next few years, describe why. Use footnotes or endnotes to support any included facts and figures.

In Microsoft Word, you can create a footnote or endnote by positioning the pointer where you want the citation to appear, clicking Insert on the menu bar, then clicking Footnote. The Word footnote and endnote feature is shown in Figure 2.5. When you have clicked the appropriate option buttons, click OK. Type the footnote/endnote information in the space provided. A completed footnote is shown in Figure 2.6.

Take Note

Vagueness indicates you have not formulated your ideas fully.

What Is the Purpose of Your Business?

Once you've discussed the industry, it's time to talk directly about your company. Include your company's **mission statement,** a short description of your purpose and target customer. Make sure your mission statement is clear.

When describing your business, you should include the following information:

- Indicate whether your business sells products or provides services. If selling products, are you a wholesaler, retailer, business-to-business, or manufacturer?

- Describe when and how the business got started, as well as its legal structure (corporation, partnership, or sole proprietorship).

- Briefly list the principals of the company and their expertise.

FIGURE 2.5

Footnote and Endnote Dialog Box

Determines location of citation

Determines numbering scheme

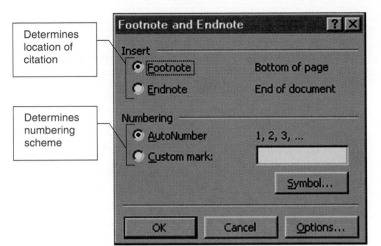

FIGURE 2.6

Completed Footnote

Solid line separates text from footnote

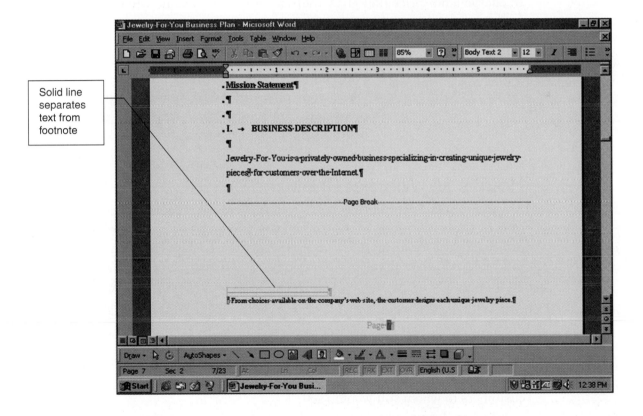

- Define what market needs you will be meeting and how your products or services will be sold.
- Determine if you will need to provide customer service, and how? Also include whether advertising and promotion will be needed.

 Think out of the box. A defined market may not already exist for your business: you may be creating one.

What Products or Services Will the Business Provide?

Each product or service you will be providing should be detailed. You should strive for giving the reader a good feel for what you are providing without bogging down in unnecessary information. Describe any end uses or applications your products will have. Be sure to mention anything unique about your product or service; these features can distinguish your business from your competitors.

In this section, you should take every opportunity to emphasize why your product or service is different from what is already available. Go into detail about what makes your business idea competitive.

Where Does the Business Fit in the Market?

Market **position,** or where your business fits within the industry, is an important identity to convey. Jewelry-For-You might position itself as a custom jeweler using only the finest gemstones. Your position should be based on the quality of your product or service, fulfillment of your customer's needs, the corporate image you want to project, and the position of your competition.

What Will I Charge Customers?

In business, you have to charge customers for your products or services. You want to charge a fair price that gives your customers good value while your business makes a profit. In addition, you also want your prices to increase acceptance of your product or service and increase your market share. This section should outline what you will charge and how you arrived at your pricing scheme. Outline also where your prices fall with your competitors. If your prices are significantly lower than those of your competitors, explain how you can afford to do this.

E-tip
Be realistic about your costs. If you underestimate your costs, you will have to raise your prices later, and this can be received negatively.

How Is My Market Analyzed?

As you formulate your business plan, you think about characteristics of your customers, the composition of the market, your competition, and your best guess of projected sales for the next few years. Each of these factors makes up the market in which you will be doing business, and a careful analysis of the market will better prepare you as you get started. Figure 2.7 contains information found on the Marketplace section in the Small Business Administration's web page.

Who Are My Customers?

Whether your business supplies products or a service, you have a particular customer in mind. In this section, you will be describing the characteristics of the customers to whom you want to sell.

When analyzing your customers, keep in mind the following:

- Are they cost or quality conscious?
- What influences them to make a purchase?
- What other concerns do they have?

Customers for Jewelry-For-You would be men and women interested in high-quality, customized jewelry, whose concern for cost is secondary to the goods they are receiving. They are probably not impulse buyers, since it takes some time to consider the design and features of the jewelry the company offers.

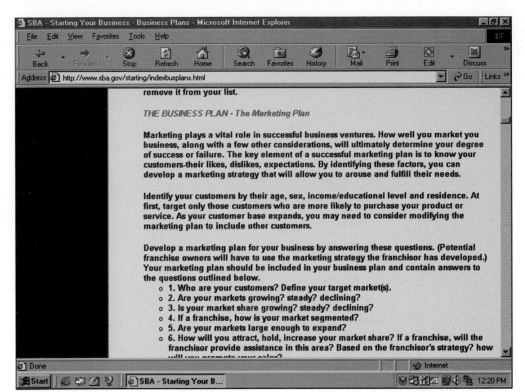

FIGURE 2.7

Marketing Information from the SBA

Is customer location a factor? In the case of an eBusiness, distance may not matter, whereas it might be a concern in a bricks-and-mortar business. Define your customers in simple, nontechnical terms, and you can also describe those customers you are not interested in reaching.

What Is the Market?

Whether your business supplies products or services, you probably have a particular market you want to reach. In this section, you will be defining the market in which your customers are found. Figure 2.8 contains a handy checklist provided on the SBA website that helps you conduct your own market analysis.

Factors affecting market growth should be discussed, and it only strengthens your case if you include factual data. Any data included should cite its source.

Who Is the Competition?

As a businessperson, you should know your competition. Know your competitors' products or services, sources of goods, distribution channels, and price structures. In this section, you can name names and briefly discuss each competitor's strengths and weaknesses.

Ask yourself why customers buy from these competitors. Is it price, convenience, customer service, quality, or reputation? Can your business offer customers something better than they are already getting?

What Are My Estimated Sales?

Of course you won't know until your business is actually operating, but you probably have a good idea of the volume of sales you plan to generate. It may be helpful

Take Note

All the individual customers occupy the market. A 40-year-old female accountant, lawyer, or physician would be a customer; the market would include professional women.

FIGURE 2.8

SBA Market Analysis
Checklist

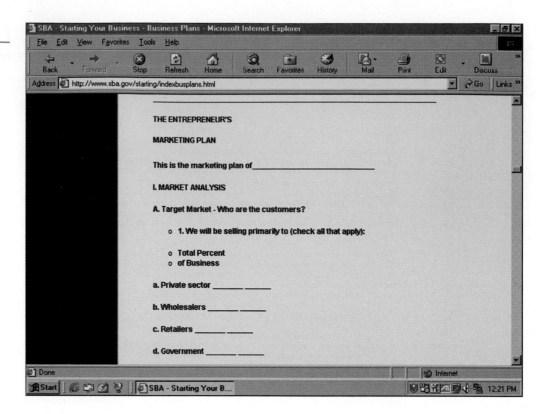

to break down this volume by unit and dollars, as well as fiscal quarters. Once you have defined your customers, the market, the advantages of your products or services, and the competition, project sales for the next three years. Back up your projections with a summary that justifies these claims, and substantiate your projections with any pertinent data.

How Is My Product/Service Produced?

Most products or services require some development period before they can be marketed and sold to the public. A business producing a product may have to create a prototype before it can be mass-produced. A service company may have to conduct market research and print materials such as stationery, business cards, and forms. As you determine the costs necessary to create the products or deliver the services, create a budget that includes all your expenses, including labor.

You can find many sample plans for specific types of businesses. Figure 2.9 shows the types of sample plans available on the Web.

How Is a Product or Service Developed?

The development process is that phase before the product or service actually exists. During this time, your business is preparing to bring the product or service to market. This might include obtaining necessary patents, trademarks, or copyrights. It's easy to see how a product is developed. A new product might have schematic drawings for a **prototype,** or model. Once the prototype is complete, it will be manufactured, either in-house or by an outsourcer in the production process.

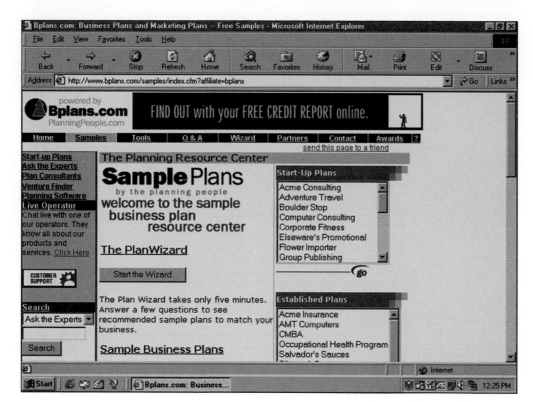

FIGURE 2.9

Examples of Sample Business Plans

The development of a service may not be so apparent. Instead of having a prototype, market research might be conducted to establish a list of potential clients, or to test the waters for the necessity of the service.

How Is a Product or Service Produced?

It is during the production process that the product or service is created. In this section, you describe the process so any reader can understand what is necessary to produce the product or service.

You may choose to produce any components you need or purchase them from an outside source—it depends on your company's product or service. You should include your choice (making or buying) and defend the reasons for your decision.

How Much Will It Cost?

The costs associated with the production of the product or service sold by your company should be outlined in this section. All the costs associated with the design and actual production should be included, including labor, materials, patent fees, and consulting and professional fees. Figure 2.10 contains informative tips on what should be included in this section.

What Are the Nonmanagerial Labor Requirements?

The production of your product or service requires a certain amount of nonmanagerial labor. Include the nonmanagerial labor that will be required to start up and run your company. In this section, you should also include the skill sets this labor pool should have, as well as current and future costs of labor. Include any training expenses that will be required.

FIGURE 2.10

Costs of Production
and Development Tips

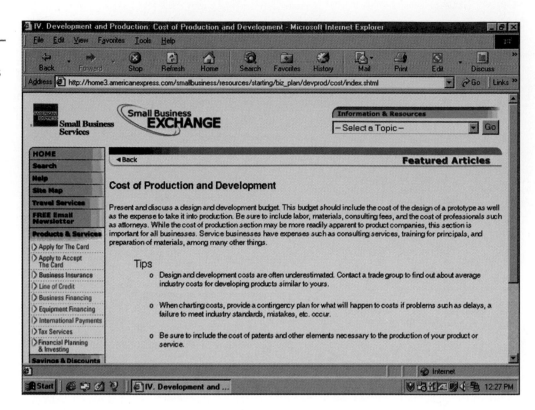

What Other Financial Information Is Necessary?

The costs associated with the production of products or services are included in the development and production section. The following information should be included in spreadsheet form:

- Operating expenses—This spreadsheet should include all expenses involved in running your business. It should contain marketing, sales, and overhead, such as administrative costs, travel expenses, equipment leases, and supplies.
- Capital requirements—This spreadsheet outlines the funds you will need to procure equipment necessary to start and run your business.
- Cost of goods—These costs are only involved in a business in which products are manufactured and sold.

What Are My Strategies?

Sales and marketing is an important part of your business plan. Although you will also be writing a marketing plan, this portion of the business plan covers key aspects of sales and marketing. This section is not meant to replace the actual marketing plan.

In this section, you define how you will find customers, marketing techniques you will use, how your product or service will be distributed, as well as your advertising and promotion campaign strategies.

How Will I Sell and Market My Products/Services?

In this section, you will tie the previous information about pricing, target customers, market, and competition, and formulate a strategy your business will use

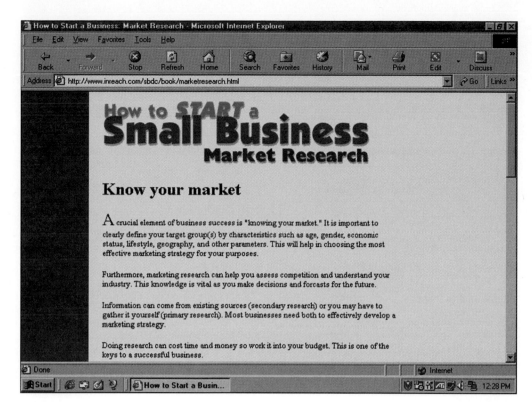

FIGURE 2.11

Small Business Market Research Information

to get customers to buy your products or services. Successful marketing tips, such as those shown in Figure 2.11, can be found on many websites.

It's important that you emphasize how you will find potential customers. Once they are located, you need to give them information that acquaints them with your business. Know the distinction between sales and marketing. Getting the product or service to customers is **sales.** Educating the consumer about your product or service is **marketing.** Emphasize the tactics you will use to make your products or services stand out from others. Be sure to mention any unique methods you will be using.

How Will I Distribute My Products/Services?

The means you use to deliver your products or services to customers are called **distribution channels.** Jewelry-For-You might arrange to have pieces sold by upscale online clothing vendors such as Sundance or J. Jill. In the case of an eBusiness, it is also important that you consider whether or not you are shipping directly to the customer, or to a go-between, such as the online merchant, who then forwards the merchandise.

How Will I Advertise and Promote My Products/Services?

Products and services are effectively marketed through advertising and promotion. Sample advertisements, such as website banners or print ads, should be included in this section. Any promotional tactics should support sales efforts and should be discussed with the people who will promote your business.

Define your sales and marketing strategies using sites such as the one shown in Figure 2.12.

FIGURE 2.12

Sales and Marketing
Strategies

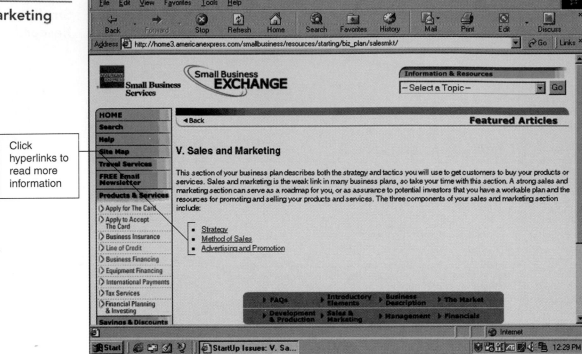

Click hyperlinks to read more information

What Staff Is Needed?

Earlier in the business plan, you detailed the type and amount of nonmanagerial labor required to make your business successful. In this section, you will describe the managerial staff, board of directors, and support services that make your business effective.

Who Is Managing the Business?

Members of your management staff should be detailed, including their names, responsibilities, and experience. In the case of positions not yet filled, list what hires remain and their responsibilities. It is more important that you have detailed knowledge of the types of people you need, rather than having those positions already filled.

Indicate if any of your employees have a history of working within your industry or with you personally. Figure 2.13 contains introductory text for the management section of a business plan.

Make sure personnel experiences are listed in reverse chronological order, and stress strengths and expertise.

Who Owns the Business?

This section should describe who maintains ownership and control of the business. It is necessary that readers understand who is making important business decisions. In cases in which you are looking for funding, a potential investor will be looking at how much equity is available.

Who Is on the Board of Directors?

A **board of directors** can add credibility to a new business; it also provides *economy of motion*. The board can steer a business in a specific direction, depending

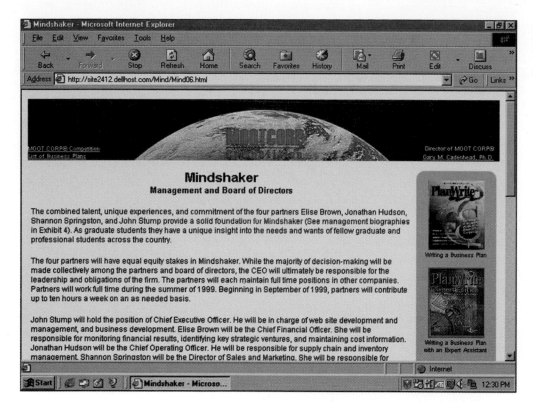

FIGURE 2.13

Sample Management
Section

on its membership. In this section, you should outline those board members already appointed, their expertise, and how each one can be beneficial.

When selecting board members, look less for friends and more for talent and direction.

Who Are My Support Services?

Not all your managerial support comes from direct hires. Some of the most important help comes from **support services,** professional advisors such as attorneys, accountants, and public relations firms. In this section, list all the support services you have retained, with a short description of their expertise and how they can be beneficial.

What Are My Financial Considerations?

As you near the conclusion of the business plan, you should be prepared to discuss the current finances of your business and the risks involved. You should be prepared to provide a cash flow statement, balance sheet, and income statement, as well as a statement of necessary funding. The types of information you should include in this section are shown in Figure 2.14.

How Do I Assess the Risks?

Every business has risk. This section should outline areas of risk and your minimization methods. Feel free to speculate here. What would you do if an advertising campaign misses its mark? What if your orders exceed your supplies? What if a supplier drastically raises prices?

THE EDGE

Be preemptive in raising these issues; it shows you are thinking ahead and are aware of potential hazards.

FIGURE 2.14

Financial Section
Information

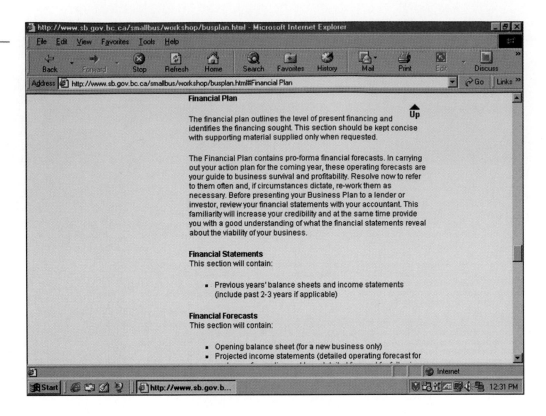

What Is the Cash Flow Statement?

A **cash flow statement** details where money comes from and how it is used. This statement, in spreadsheet form, should be a realistic look at your business expenditures and revenues. Make sure you take into account any seasonal shifts, and show monthly figures. Offer explanations of any unusually large or small values in the report. Tips for preparing a cash flow statement are also found on the Web, as shown in Figure 2.15.

What Is the Balance Sheet?

A **balance sheet** calculates the net worth of a business. This report, generally created on an annual basis, summarizes assets and liabilities within the business. In addition to including the report, offer an analysis that explains any important events that occurred.

What Is the Income Statement?

The **income statement** details revenue, expenses, capital, and costs of goods and reflects the amount of money your business makes or loses within a year. Unlike the cash flow statement, the income statement summarizes revenues and expenses but does not indicate when these transactions occurred.

How Much Money Do I Need?

At the conclusion of the business plan, outline exactly how much money you think your business needs, what type of funding you want, and when you want it. If you want money in stages, indicate how the money will help advance the business and how it will be used.

Although you want to be positive, provide an exit strategy that indicates how any investors will be able to recoup their money in the event of a business failure.

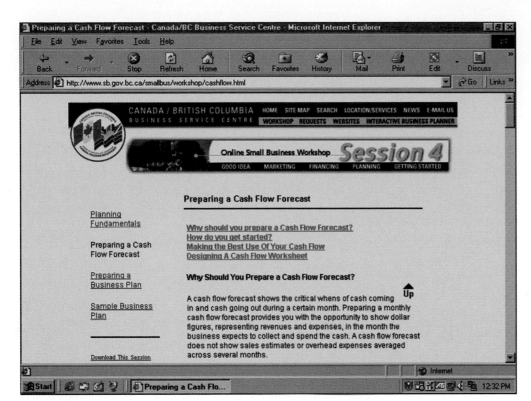

FIGURE 2.15

Cash Flow Statement Tips

Checkpoint

The dreaded business plan can be your best friend. Although it involves a lot of research, time, and effort, this is the document that can reassure you that your business idea has merit and can succeed. As you complete each section, you should be more confident than ever in your goals.

In addition, your business plan can open the door to financial backing and can be used to attract the quality people and businesses you want associated with your company. Each section within a business plan contains information vital to making your business come alive. The key elements are listed below, although you may see different section titles and organization elsewhere.

- Executive summary (part of the introduction)
- Business description
- Marketplace
- Development and production
- Sales and marketing
- Management
- Financial information

Keys

angels	mission statement	board of directors
venture capitalists	position	support services
strategic partners	prototype	cash flow statement
executive summary	sales	balance sheet
business description	marketing	income statement
industry	distribution channels	

Milestones

Complete the following statements:

1. The _____ _____ section provides an overview of the entire business plan.
2. A(n) _____ _____ is a business with whom you form an alliance and work jointly.
3. The _____ _____ is a brief description of your company's purpose and target customer.
4. Where your business fits within its industry is called market _____.
5. A model of your intended product is called a(n) _____.
6. _____ involves educating the consumer about your products or services.
7. _____ _____ determine the way in which products and services are delivered to your customers.
8. The _____ _____ _____ can add credibility to a business and determine its direction.
9. Professional advisors, such as accountants, are your _____ _____.
10. The net worth of a business is calculated in the _____ _____.

Complete the following exercises:

1. Locate several web sources of business plan information, noting their URLs. Which of these sources do you prefer? Why?
2. For whom is a business plan written?

Your Turn

Assume you are about to start an eBusiness using either a real-life example or a fictitious product or service company. Open a new document using your favorite word processor and save it as Business Plan Outline. Create an outline containing probable contents of a business plan. For example, while you would not actually be locating potential customers, speculate who they might be and where they would be located.

CHAPTER 3

Promoting

Why Do I Need a Marketing Plan?

Jeremy never cared for sales, but he always recognized its importance. Now on the verge of starting his own eBusiness, an online service that locates rare stamps, he understands the importance of sales and marketing.

He always knew his idea would work, but it was always hard to verbalize his plan to others. Now that his business plan is complete and he has interested financial backers, he has to produce a marketing plan that shows how he will make his dream company a reality. After all, it doesn't matter if you have a great idea for a business if you don't have any customers. The marketing plan will solidify the identity of the target customers and detail how Jeremy can reach—and entice—his potential customers.

Developing a Marketing Plan

CHAPTER OUTLINE

Why Is a Marketing Plan Necessary?

How Do I Start the Marketing Plan?

What Factors Influence My Business?

Who Are My Target Customers?

What Are the Advantages of My Product or Service?

What Are My Marketing Tactics?

How Can I Calculate a Marketing Budget?

Why Will My Business Succeed?

FIGURE 3.1

Planning

Why Is a Marketing Plan Necessary?

While the goal of your business might be to make a lot of money, to accomplish this you need to have a plan. The plan you implement will be based on the products or services your business provides, the market you want to reach, and how you intend to reach them.

Like the business plan, the marketing plan is a road map for reaching your objectives of bringing your business products or services to the public. There are a variety of organizational schemes used in marketing plans, but ultimately they all cover similar information. Table 3.1 contains information categories and contents typically included in a marketing plan.

You can search the Web to find samples and hints about writing a marketing plan. Figure 3.2 shows results of such a search.

How Is the Marketing Plan Used?

What will you do, when will you do it? These are typical marketing questions. Because marketing is oriented around strategy, you can use a marketing plan as a means of detailing your actions and avoiding potential problems. By writing a marketing plan, you can hope to achieve the following:

TABLE 3.1

Typical Marketing Plan Ingredients

Category	Contents
Introduction	The cover page
	Table of contents
	Executive summary
Situational analysis	Examine demand and trends in the environment
	Determine your position in the industry
	Determine the impact of groups or organizations
	Describe the competition
	Define the environment within your company
Target customers	Determine the demographics of your customers
	Describe the buying habits of your customers
	Know what your customers want
Advantages and disadvantages	Describe positive and negative aspects
	Define how they will be addressed
Marketing tactics	List how you intend to reach target customers
	Describe your marketing methods
	Detail your marketing mix
	Describe how you will implement the plan
Marketing budget	Determine how much money is needed
	Describe how you can achieve these monetary goals
Summary	Discuss why your plan will be a success

Your search results may differ

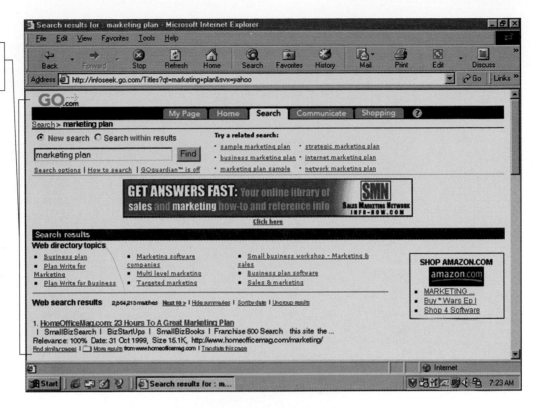

FIGURE 3.2

Marketing Plan Search Results

- Chart your goals and objectives.
- Implement your strategy.
- Determine roles and responsibilities.
- Acquire resources when needed.
- Utilize resources efficiently.
- Predict and circumvent problems.

THE EDGE

The business plan summarizes the entire company; the marketing plan zeros in on how the company will reach its goals.

How Do I Start the Marketing Plan?

In the business plan, the executive summary summarizes the plan. In the marketing plan, the **executive summary** provides a synopsis of your marketing strategies. It's unfortunate, but some people may only read the executive summary, so it is vital that this section of the marketing plan should stand on its own.

 Including an executive summary makes it easy for a reader to find the highlights without having to read an entire document.

Since you will probably be writing the introductory information last—as you did in the business plan—you might want to leave several pages in the report for the cover page, executive summary, and table of contents.

Consider offering your business and marketing plans in electronic format to interested parties.

To give consistency to the business and marketing plan, you may want to use the same visual format. This way, both reports will look like companions.

BUSINESS *Gift*

PASSWORD-PROTECTING A DOCUMENT

In this age of online activity, some readers may prefer to view your business or marketing plans in electronic form. While most word processors can open most text-processed files, you may be more concerned about protecting your documents from theft or modification. Microsoft Word, for example, supplies several tools you can use to prevent document tampering. Among your options are

- **Requiring a password to open a document.** Only those people with a password would be able to open the document. In Word, click File on the menu bar, click Save As, then click Options. The Save dialog box opens, as shown in Figure 3.3. Type a password in the Password to open text box, click OK, then click Save.

- **Requiring a password to modify a document.** Anyone could open the document, but a password would be necessary to make and save modifications. In Word, click File on the menu bar, click Save As, then click Options. Type a password in the Password to modify text box, click OK, then click Save.

- **Saving a document in read-only format.** Changes can be saved only if the document is saved using another name. In Word, click File on the menu bar, click Save As, then click Options. Select the Read-only recommended checkbox, click OK, then click Save.

- **Protect a document by assigning a password.** Password-protection allows comments and tracked changes but prevents other modifications. In Word, click Tools on the menu bar, then Protect Document. The Protect Document dialog box opens, as shown in Figure 3.4. Select the option buttons for the types of protection you want, type an optional password, if necessary, then click OK.

What Factors Influence My Business?

THE EDGE

In this section, you should be examining the environment in which your business will be operating and thinking about factors that might affect it positively or negatively.

The section following the executive summary is called the situational analysis. The **situational analysis** provides information on various environments affecting your business. Prior to this section, you might want to include one or more explanatory paragraphs explaining the purpose of your business. This introduction is different from the executive summary, as it is not an overview.

An introduction provides text that will ease your readers into the situational analysis information. Without this transitional text, the situational analysis information might seem abrupt and disjointed.

Within the situational analysis, there are four factors you should examine:

- Situational environment, in which you examine current and potential demands and trends.
- Neutral environment, in which you determine the impact of groups or organizations.
- Competitor environment, in which you describe the competition.
- Company environment, in which you define the environment within your company.

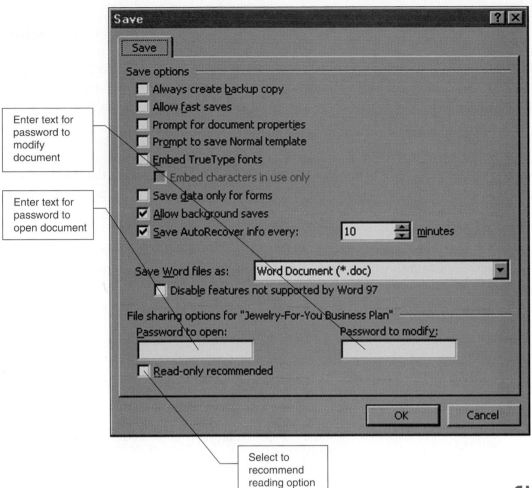

Enter text for password to modify document

Enter text for password to open document

Select to recommend reading option

FIGURE 3.3

Save Dialog Box

FIGURE 3.4

Protect Document Dialog Box

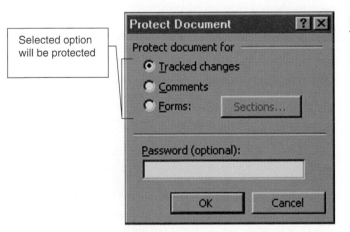

Selected option will be protected

What Are the Demands and Trends?

You've probably thought of how your business can grow. Ideally, your company will take off and grow as you get new customers and expand your base. The analysis of current and potential demand allows you to determine how large your business should be when you start and lets you plan its potential size.

If your business concept is strong, demand should increase as more people experience your products or services.

Who Makes the Decisions?

Part of assessing demand and trends is determining who makes the purchase and who makes the purchase decision. They are not always the same person. Once you know who makes the purchase decision—and obtain some demographic information—you can determine how to reach that audience.

For example, if the decision maker or purchaser tends to belong to a particular business organization, you might try to obtain that organization's mailing list or e-mail list and contact those people.

THE EDGE

Consider factors other than ethnicity; look for any commonalities among decision makers.

Is My Business Affected by Groups and Organizations?

Although your customers may be individuals or businesses, take an objective look at whether or not groups or organizations have an effect on your business. Is your business politically correct? Could popular opinion work in your favor or against you? Could government regulations have a positive or negative impact?

Take Note

If any groups could adversely affect your business, you should have a strategy to counter this.

Who Are My Competitors?

You should always know your competitors. Know their strengths and weaknesses, as well as their suppliers, distribution channels, and market niches. Know how they are similar to your business, and know how they are different. You should also be familiar with your competitors' strategies; analyze their relative effectiveness. The site shown in Figure 3.5 contains information helpful to analyzing your competition.

Learn from your competition; they have something to teach you.

Business Gift — EMBEDDING COMMENTS IN A DOCUMENT

It would be difficult for a single person to write the business plan or marketing plan, much less both documents. At the very least, you'll probably want several pairs of eyes to read the text and make comments.

If your readers or co-authors want to examine a document in Microsoft Word, each contributor can embed comments directly in the document. There is no limit to the number of contributors who can make comments, and each comment is identified numerically and with user initials. A comment is placed at the pointer location when the command is given and can also be applied to multiple words, as shown in Figure 3.6. To embed a comment, position the pointer at the location for the comment either by clicking a location or selecting text, click Insert on the menu bar, then click Comment. The Comment window automatically opens at the lower portion of the screen revealing the next consecutive number and the initials of the user. Type your comments, then click Close.

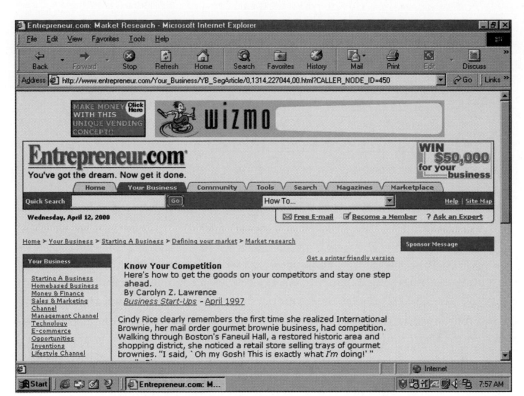

FIGURE 3.5

Analyzing Your
Competition

FIGURE 3.6

Comment Embedded
in Document

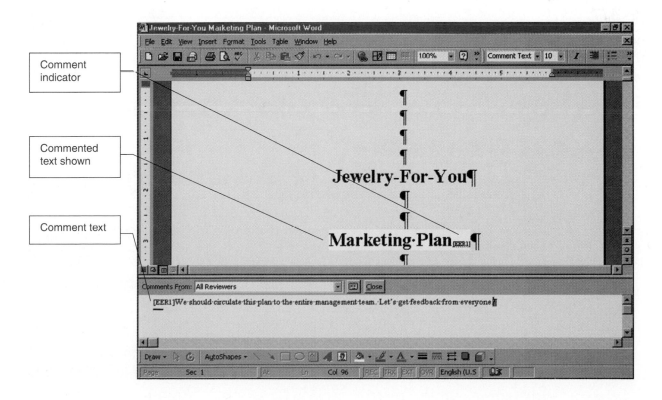

What Is My Corporate Climate?

You should objectively and critically examine the climate within your own company. What sort of culture exists? Understand the resources available within the company and the nature of your relationships with customers and suppliers. It might be beneficial to write the strengths and weaknesses that exist.

Who Are My Target Customers?

THE EDGE

Some marketing plan topics may appear repetitive. While the territory may be similar, each section should include a different perspective.

To market to your customers successfully, you need to know more about them. If you are an online clothing retailer, for example, you'll probably want a more in-depth description than "my customers are people who wear clothes." Figure 3.7 shows a site that contains information that can help you define your target customers.

As you define your target customers, you will probably begin to separate your potential customers into segments. An example of a segment would be homeowners or vacationers. Members of each **segment** have common characteristics that allow you to focus your marketing efforts toward a particular group. When determining segments, think about the relative population of each group; this will give you perspective on where you should concentrate your marketing efforts—and dollars.

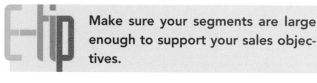

Make sure your segments are large enough to support your sales objectives.

There are many ways of identifying customers demographically. Using research—either self-generated or purchased from organizations—you can find out about your customers. Don't guess; information can be purchased at relatively low costs and can pay large dividends.

FIGURE 3.7

Determining Target
Customers

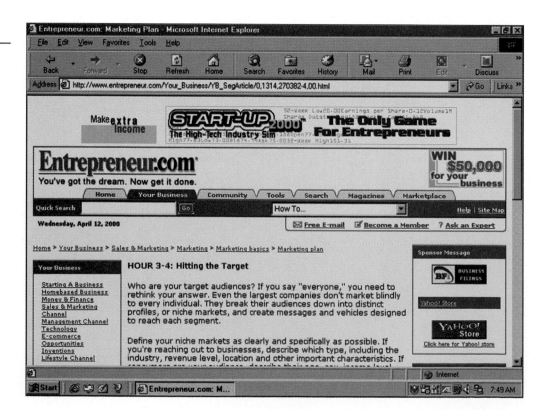

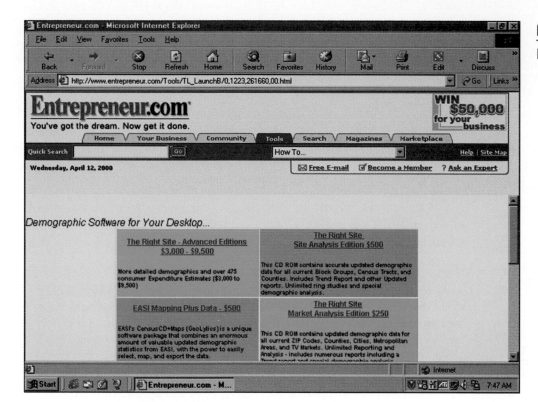

FIGURE 3.8

Demographic Services

As you analyze your target markets, think of characteristics shared by your customers:

- What are their **demographics** (age, income, ethnicity, and education)? Are there any commonalties between segments? Figure 3.8 contains a website offering demographic services.
- Where are they located? Is this a factor in marketing your product or service?
- What marketing psychology might work on your target customers? Do they appreciate humor in their advertising? Do they dislike a hard-sell approach? Can they take a joke?
- What type of lifestyle do your target customers enjoy?

What Are the Advantages of My Product or Service?

While everyone loves to discuss their strengths, there is little enjoyment to be found in uncovering our weaknesses. Yet, like people, all businesses have them. In this section, you will be restating any strengths and weaknesses discussed in earlier sections.

Why Should I Bring up Problem Areas?

Quite simply, if you don't discuss potential problems, someone else will. Failure to disclose possible problems makes you appear myopic and may raise questions about your judgment. Also, when you bring up a negative aspect, you have the opportunity to discuss it rationally and on your own terms. If you neglect to address problems, you may appear defensive when presented with it by others. You can

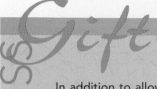

ANNOTATING A DOCUMENT

In addition to allowing readers to add comments in your document, they can also make modifications—additions, deletions, and rearrangements of text—without actually making these changes final. This feature is called **tracking** and displays changes in a different color and with a vertical line displayed to the left of the text. Figure 3.9 contains a document that has been edited by multiple reviewers and also has footnotes and comments. As you make final editing decisions, you can choose to accept or reject any of these changes as you see fit.

To control tracking options, click Tools on the menu bar, point to Track Changes, then click Highlight Changes. Selecting the Track Changes while editing checkbox displays all modifications in the document.

Once the settings have been chosen, the tracking feature can be turned on and off using a toggle switch on the status. A **toggle switch** is a button or command that is turned on or off using the same action, much like a light switch. To turn tracking on, double-click the TRK box in the Microsoft Word status bar. To turn tracking off, double-click TRK. When it does not display, the feature is off. When TRK displays, the tracking feature is on. You can accept or reject a change by right-clicking the change, then clicking Accept Change or Reject Change.

FIGURE 3.9

Annotated Text

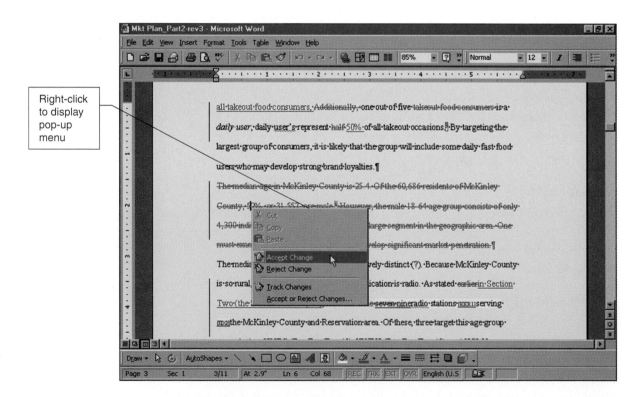

Right-click to display pop-up menu

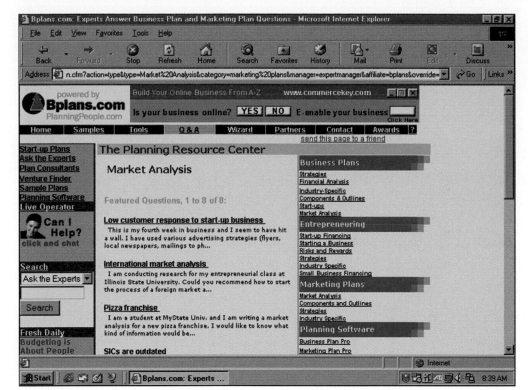

FIGURE 3.10

Answers to Common Business Problems

find answers to many common business problems at sites such as the one shown in Figure 3.10.

The ability to recognize problems within your industry and company means you can look objectively at your business. This quality is the mark of a good businessperson and a leader.

What Is My Industry Position?

As you determine the advantages and disadvantages of your business, you'll define your identity, or **position,** in the market. Ultimately, position is based upon the perception others have of your business. Initially, this position will be based on your marketing. Once your business is established, it will be based on a combination of marketing and how well you equal or exceed your claims or deliver the goods.

You should base your positioning on the positive aspects of your products or services. Consider the following when thinking about how your business can be positioned:

- Create a statement that describes your business position. Use descriptive adjectives that measure your products or services in the most glowing terms. See Figure 3.11 for additional positioning tips.

- Try to locate a market niche that has not yet been filled. Use this information in your position statement.

- Emphasize your strengths; avoid basing position on pricing. A price advantage can be short-lived and can change quickly.

- Claims should be based on substance. If customers find your promises are superficial, they will not be around for long.

FIGURE 3.11

Positioning Tips

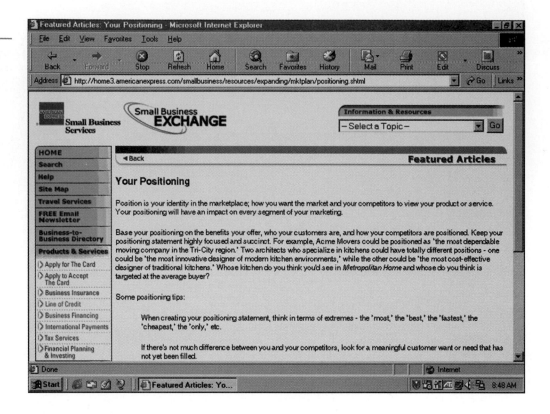

What Are My Marketing Tactics?

Understanding the strengths and weaknesses of your products or services makes it possible to develop a marketing strategy. Marketing strategies are based on **tactics:** the measures you take to make your strategies a reality. Marketing strategy questions are addressed in various websites, such as the one shown in Figure 3.12.

In marketing, there are a variety of tools at your disposal. Some of these tools are listed in the website shown in Figure 3.13.

What Should I Consider When Developing Marketing Tactics?

Before you can develop marketing tactics, you need to consider several factors that influence the current state of the market. These factors include the following:

- The size of the market, its growth potential, and the level of demand. This will also help you determine how you price your products or services.
- The availability of materials necessary to your business.
- Barriers to entry to you, your competitors, and your customers. Will it be difficult for you to get started in this business? Will it be difficult for your competitors to compete? Will it be easy for potential customers to begin working with you?
- The life cycle of your products or services. Can your products or services sustain growth and mature? Is the life cycle long enough that your business can recoup its investments? Do you have other products or services in the pipeline to augment or replace your current line? **Pipeline** is a metaphor for the process needed to bring a product or service from idea inception to reality.

THE EDGE

Depending on a single product or service is risky for any business. It's a good idea to always have a new product or service in the pipeline to replace or augment lackluster offerings. Additional offerings are a good hedge against a shift in the marketplace.

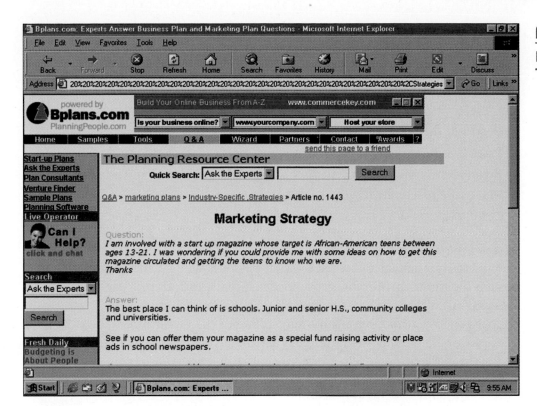

FIGURE 3.12

Marketing Strategy
Topics

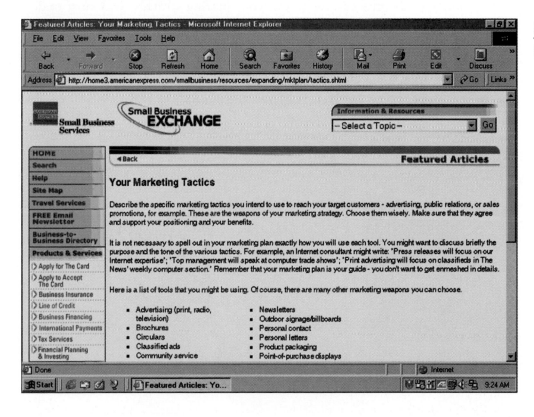

FIGURE 3.13

Marketing Tools

How Do I Develop Tactics?

The subject of marketing tactics is neatly divided into four categories: product, price, promotion, and place. Each of these categories, shown in Figure 3.14, represents elements that you can somewhat control. This **marketing mix,** also known as the four Ps, includes the following:

- **Product:** the goods or services your business brings to the marketplace.
- **Price:** what you charge your customers.
- **Promotion:** how you present your goods and services to entice customers.
- **Place:** the mechanisms you use to get your goods and services to your customers.

What Is the Product?

The product or service delivered by each business will differ, but some features remain the same. Any product or service is initially introduced, can be modified, and may ultimately be withdrawn from the market. Circumstances under your control—or beyond your control—may influence the time between these events.

For example, your competitors may introduce new products that compel you to enhance an existing product or come out with a new product line.

How Should I Price My Product/Service?

Naturally you want customers to buy your product or service, but you don't want to lose money in the process. As part of your pricing strategy, you must understand when you will receive the money you collect.

Some businesses, such as restaurants, often collect cash. In these cases, a large portion of the business revenue is immediate. In an eBusiness, however, most of your online transactions will be paid with credit cards. If so, know the lag time between transaction and when you will receive your money. During that time, you

FIGURE 3.14

Marketing Mix

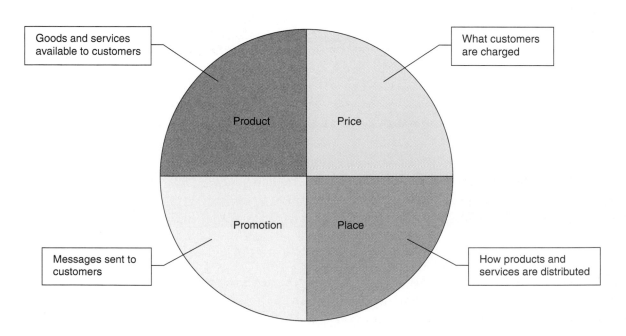

must deliver the product or service and may incur charges such as shipping. Until you are paid, you will be bearing these costs.

Customers can be fickle when it comes to price. Charge too much and they may think you're trying to take advantage. Charge too little and they may suspect the quality. Your price should be just right: low enough to entice, reasonable for its quality, and enabling you to cover your expenses and make a profit. You can always use short-term price promotions such as sales, coupons, and other incentives to tempt customers.

Look down the line at the evolution of the market when determining price strategies. Take into consideration all the costs associated with the marketing mix.

How Do I Promote My Business?

The way in which you promote the intentions of your business generally has a direct effect on sales. The levels of communication widely used include advertising, public relations, sales efforts, and reaching out to potential customers.

Ideally, you want customers to think of you first. Your business should be at the top of a customer's mental list.

Regardless of the method of promotion, the goal is to entice the customer to buy your product or service. To achieve this goal, you may choose to expose potential customers to your business name whenever possible.

There are three basic objectives of promotion: to inform, persuade, and remind. This means that your promotional strategy is not to advertise only when you have a sale, but to *inform* them about what you do and why your function is necessary. Once you have educated customers of the necessity of your product or service, you can *persuade* them that they stand to gain from your business. Constant *reminders* reinforce your existence to the customer.

How Will My Customers Buy from Me?

As an eBusiness, it is reasonable to expect that your customers will make purchases from you online. In most cases, they will probably buy products or services from you using your website, although you may also offer customers telephone access through a toll-free number.

Find links that help you learn more about enabler software at the website for this book.

EBusinesses that sell customized products often rely on sophisticated software that enables the customer to pick and choose options to create a specific, personalized product.

How Can I Calculate a Marketing Budget?

Most businesses want to get spectacular marketing results while spending as little as possible. Unfortunately, marketing is expensive, and its results are not immediately realized. Some marketing effects are realized over long periods of time and are difficult to measure precisely.

There are four methods of determining the size of your marketing budget. These methods are also discussed in the website shown in Figure 3.15.

- Create a budget based on an agreed-upon percentage of previous or projected sales. While this method creates a realistic budget for current production, it does not account for shifts in the marketplace; it assumes a direct relationship between marketing expenditures and sales results.

ENABLING SOFTWARE

There are a lot of companies out there that make eBusiness transactions happen, and you've probably never heard of them. These companies, called **enablers,** are building the infrastructure that makes eCommerce work in the retail and business-to-business (B2B) worlds. Working behind the scenes, these companies provide an operations backbone in which eBusinesses function. Some enabler technologies help companies manage their web content, while others help configure products.

Some eBusinesses are so complex, they use multiple enabler software programs.

Still others make it possible for transactions to take place.

However, before a transaction can happen, you must *lure the customer.* Once the customer is at your website, you must *provide relevant content.* The customer can *receive customized goods while utilizing self-service.*

There are five primary types of enabling software: content management, product configuration, transaction platforms, supply-chain management, and data mining.

- *Content management* assembles and categorizes product information and is primarily used by catalog eBusinesses.
- *Product configuration* software makes it possible to create build-to-order products within a website and is often used by computer hardware manufacturers.
- *Transaction platforms* are used to match buyers' and sellers' bids in Internet marketplaces and are used in online auctions.
- *Supply-chain management* allows inventories to be controlled, aids in monitoring fulfillment systems, and is utilized by large-scale manufacturers.
- *Data mining* tracks, collects, and analyzes the results of consumer behavior, such as questionnaires and purchasing selections. This technique is often used by online consumer retailers.

- Estimate your competitors' budgets. Like any estimate, this strategy can work well unless your guesses are wrong. You might be way off in your speculations, and you might not know what tactics your competitors are using.
- Spend whatever you can afford. This seat-of-the-pants approach is dangerous because you still have to operate your business and can't afford to throw all your money at marketing.
- Set dollar amounts on specific aspects of your marketing strategy. In such a strategy, there are specific tasks you want to accomplish, and you can allocate funds for each milestone. Pricing techniques are described in Figure 3.16.

What Should I Do?

Most businesses will probably hire an outside source to advise and arrange for marketing. This is a good first step, as marketing consultants will know what to do and when to do it. They will also have a good idea of how much money you will have to spend and can probably help you prepare a budget.

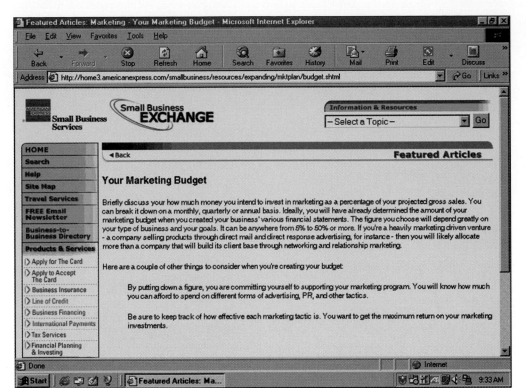

FIGURE 3.15
Budgeting Methods

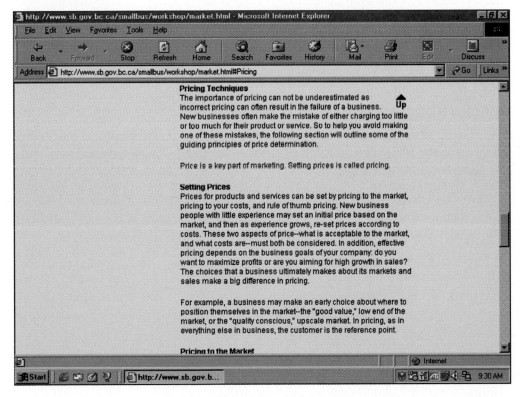

FIGURE 3.16
Pricing Techniques

Why Will My Business Succeed?

Does having a good marketing plan ensure the success of your business? Unfortunately, it doesn't. Your eBusiness should succeed if you have a sound marketing plan that is diligently implemented. Your marketing plan is a road map, and assuming the plan is sound, you should stick to it.

FIGURE 3.17

Answers to Marketing Questions

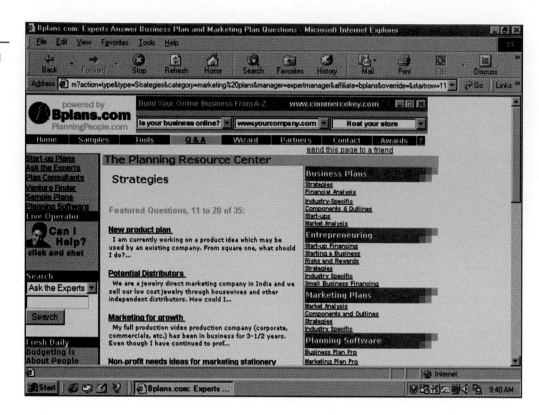

This is not to say that you have to carry out every aspect of the plan even if you find it is inappropriate. It is to say that your plan was carefully developed, and you shouldn't just ignore it. You can find answers to questions that can ensure your success in websites such as Figure 3.17.

How Do I Implement the Marketing Plan?

It would be unfortunate to go through all the work of developing a marketing plan, then have it fail during the implementation phase. There are some steps you can take to assure its success.

- Assign a person to be responsible for the implementation of the plan. This person does not have to do everything, but he or she should be empowered to delegate responsibility for specific tasks and should have the resources necessary to get the job done.

- Every task within the marketing plan should be tracked to see if expectations are met. Record results—both positive and negative—and review them frequently. If necessary, make changes to the marketing plan to accommodate your findings.

- Examine the environment within your industry. Perhaps your actions are causing unanticipated reactions in the industry that could lead you to change your marketing plans.

While overwhelming, it can be very exciting to develop a strategy that takes your eBusiness from idea to reality. The marketing plan is a detailed outline of how your business will be introduced to the public, as well as the strategies you'll use to accomplish this task.

Writing the marketing plan helps you determine who your customers are and what they want. Implementing the marketing plan makes your business a reality by bringing customers to you in a planned fashion. The key elements found in a marketing plan are listed below, although these sections often have different titles and may be ordered differently.

- Executive summary (part of the introduction)
- Situational analysis
- Target customers
- Advantages and disadvantages
- Marketing tactics
- Marketing budget
- Summary

Keys

executive summary	toggle switch	product
situational analysis	position	price
segment	tactics	promotion
demographics	pipeline	place
tracking	marketing mix	enablers

Milestones

Complete the following statements:

1. Members of each _____ have common characteristics that can be used in the marketing process.
2. Age, income, ethnicity, and education are used to describe a segment's _____.
3. You can see additions and deletions made within a document using Word's _____ feature.
4. Your identity, or _____, is based on the positive aspects of your business.
5. _____ are the measures you take to make your marketing strategies a reality.
6. The four components that make up marketing tactics are called the _____ _____.
7. The methods you use to present your goods and services to customers is called _____.
8. The three elements of promotional strategy are to inform, _____, and remind.
9. _____ are companies that build the infrastructure that makes eCommerce work.
10. Collecting and analyzing the results of consumer behavior is called _____ _____.

Complete the following exercises:

1. Locate several web sources of marketing plan information, noting their URLs. Which of these sources do you prefer? Why?
2. Which component of the marketing mix do you feel is the most important? Why?

Your Turn

Your city has hired you to write the marketing plan for a new online community college. Open a new document using your favorite word processor and save it as Marketing Mix Outline. Use your knowledge of your local area to outline the marketing mix in a few paragraphs. Each geographical area has its own unique qualities; be sure to include them in your outline.

CHAPTER 4

How Do I Design a Web Page?

Like most things in life, planning increases the odds of success. This is certainly true when it comes to website design. You don't have to be a computer wizard or graphic designer to create a great website. You do need common sense, an objective eye, and a clear idea of what you want for those who visit your site.

Kim has never designed a website, but she has a good understanding of what she wants in her Jewelry-For-You site. For the past few weeks, she has been looking critically at a lot of websites. She has been taking notes when she sees features she likes, as well as those she doesn't like. She plans on starting slow. She'll review the basics of design and then try to set up a simple entry page for her site.

Designing a Web Page

CHAPTER OUTLINE

How Do I Design an Effective Web Page?

How Do I Format Text?

What Should I Know about Graphic Design?

How Can I Use Color?

How Should I Design a Form?

How Can I Create a Website for My Business?

Where Can I Find Web Design Resources?

What Should I Consider for Special Needs Audiences?

FIGURE 4.1

Creating the Design

How Do I Design an Effective Web Page?

There are as many opinions about good web page design as there are web pages. When deciding if a page is well designed, consider first the purpose of the website. A site selling memorabilia will probably have a different atmosphere than a site for a law firm. Your first consideration should be your readers. Who are they? What will they like?

You want your readers to find your site pleasant to read and easy to navigate. If you are conducting business over your website, you want customer actions to be simple to understand, intuitive, and foolproof. Your goal should also be to provide something extra to site visitors. This something extra can be as simple as providing links to other sites that may be of interest. Adding value to your site tells customers you want to give them useful content.

E-tip Your website should be updated frequently—every few weeks—to keep it from becoming stale. A constantly changing website will draw more visitors.

There are, however, certain design standards that most business websites observe. These design elements are not etched in stone, but they make pages easier to read and, therefore, easier to navigate.

- **Keep it simple.** Strive for a clean, uncluttered look. Too many dazzling effects can confuse and overwhelm your readers. Make sure text is large enough to be read and contains no unnecessary words. Think of your own attention span. Do you spend time reading verbose websites? Make use of **white space,** those areas on the page that contain no text or graphics. The unused portions of a page do more than take up space. White space provides relief to the reader and frames the page. Imagine how cluttered a page would look if every spot had characters or images? Figure 4.2 shows the home page

FIGURE 4.2

Sample Home Page

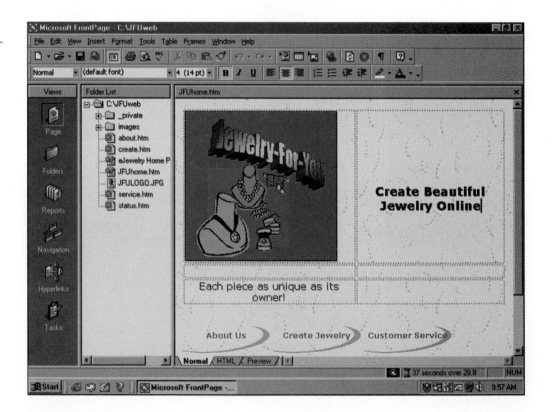

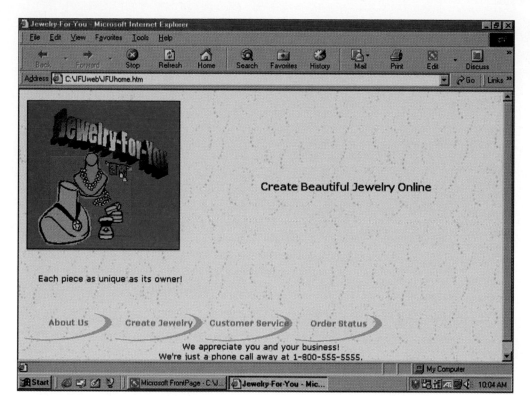

FIGURE 4.3

Sample Home Page in Browser

for the Jewelry-For-You website. Notice the subtle pattern in the background and the sparse text. At the bottom of the page, a navigation bar is provided to make it easy for the reader to go elsewhere in the site.

- **Preview the pages.** As your design progresses, you should view the pages in your browser. By doing this, you'll see the pages as your readers will see them. Figure 4.3 shows the Jewelry-For-You home page in Internet Explorer 5. If you wait until your pages are finished, you could be in for some unwelcome surprises. Make sure you—and another pair of eyes—have proofed the text for misspellings and incorrect usage. Your website text should be perfect.

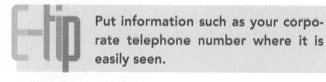

Put information such as your corporate telephone number where it is easily seen.

- **Make it easy.** Your website should be easy for a reader to understand. Information should be organized logically and should not be a treasure hunt. A **navigation bar,** buttons or links that enable readers to jump to pages within the site, should be prominently placed and easy to understand.

If possible, view your pages using a different browser to ensure that effects and features work as you expect.

- **Use good taste.** You never know who is reading your website, and you never know what someone will find offensive. Limit your text to simple, conventional phrasing, avoiding any controversial words or topics.

How Do I Format Text?

As you create a web page, you'll add descriptive text. As in any document, text that looks the same is boring and loses its impact. You'll probably want some text

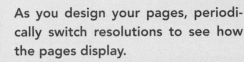

DISPLAY ISSUES

If you've ever looked at computers in other homes or offices, you may have noticed that some screens seem to display more content than others. This difference in display is due to the **resolution** (the number of pixels per inch) setting being used. The image in Figure 4.4 shows a display using a resolution of 640 × 480, whereas the images in Figures 4.2 and 4.3 use a resolution of 800 × 600. A lower resolution displays text and images larger but shows less information on the screen; a higher resolution shows more information but in a smaller size. Text and images in a higher resolution tend to be crisper than in a lower resolution. Why should this concern you? Because as a good designer, you want to know what your readers will see and how they'll see it. If you want to minimize the amount of scrolling per page, you'll design your pages in a lower resolution. Currently, many people use a resolution of 800 × 600, so this is probably safe to use in the design phase.

tip As you design your pages, periodically switch resolutions to see how the pages display.

FIGURE 4.4

640 × 480 Resolution

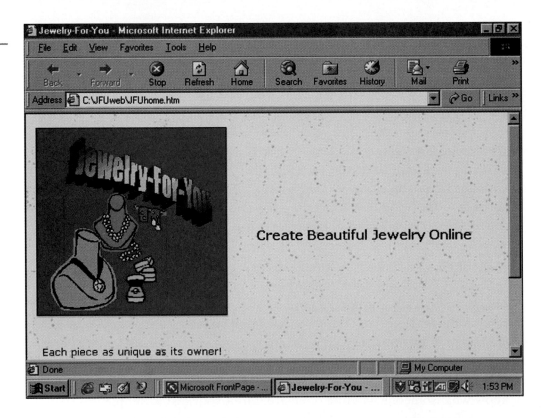

in a page to be larger than other text. Changing the appearance of text is called **formatting.** Text can be formatted by changing its typeface, or **font,** and by adding **attributes** such as bold, underline, or italics. You can also change the alignment of text and graphics using buttons on the toolbar. **Alignment** determines the location of text and graphics relative to the left margin.

There are many software programs you can use to create a web page. One such program is Microsoft FrontPage 2000. You can use features within FrontPage to quickly create a web page.

Steps

1. Click **Start** [Start] on the taskbar, point to **Programs,** then click **Microsoft FrontPage.**

   FrontPage opens displaying a new blank document. There are two toolbars visible at the top of the screen: the Standard and Formatting toolbars. The **Standard toolbar** contains buttons that are used for housekeeping operations, such as saving and printing files. Buttons on the **Formatting toolbar** are used to change the appearance of text, such as applying attributes and changing font size. The three tabs at the bottom of the page allow you to see different views of the document, and the Normal tab (the default) is currently displayed. To keep the information aligned, you can use a table as a guide to placing text and graphics.

2. Click **Insert Table** [icon] on the standard toolbar, drag the pointer from the top left square to second column in the third row, as shown in Figure 4.5, then release the mouse button. A table containing two columns and three

FIGURE 4.5

Using the Insert Table Button

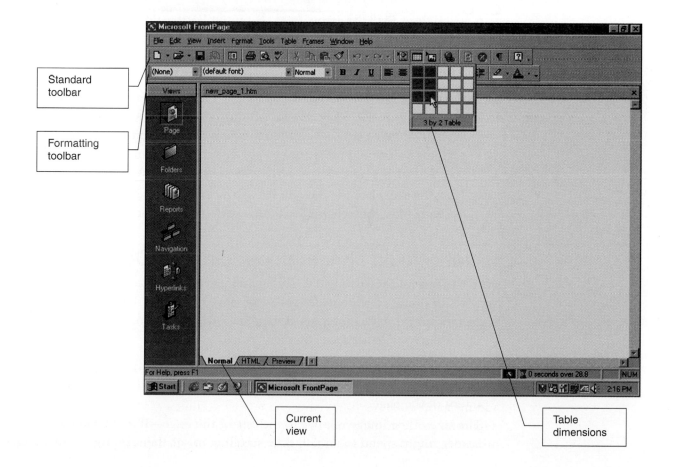

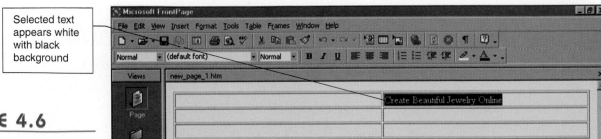

Selected text
appears white
with black
background

FIGURE 4.6

Selected Text

rows appears in the page. You can add text to the table by clicking the mouse pointer in a cell and typing.

3. Click the **upper right cell,** then type **Create Beautiful Jewelry Online.** The text appears in the cell. You can use toolbar buttons to make the text bold and change its alignment within the cell. You can format existing text by selecting it, then applying the attributes you want.

4. Press and hold the mouse button, then drag the **pointer** I so all four words are selected, as shown in Figure 4.6. The **default,** or normal, color of text is black. When black text is selected, the characters appear to be white set against a black background.

5. Click **Bold** B on the Formatting toolbar, then click **Center** ☰ on the Formatting toolbar. You can change the size of the text using a list arrow on the Formatting toolbar. Since the text is already selected, you can just use the list arrow to change the size.

6. Click **Font Size** list arrow Normal ▼ on the Formatting toolbar, click **4 (14 pt),** then click the **top left cell.** The text appears larger and is no longer selected. The pointer is now in the top left cell. To make sure your work is preserved, you can save it using a button on the Standard toolbar.

7. Click **Save** 🖫 on the Standard toolbar. The Save As dialog box opens, as seen in Figure 4.7. The text typed in the table appears as the Page title and in the File name text box. Although you want to keep the page title as it is, perhaps you would rather use a shorter file name. Since the File name text box is already selected, you can just type the new text.

8. Type **Create,** click the **Save in** list arrow to locate the approved location for your files, then click **Save.** Your work is saved and can be used later.

What Should I Know about Graphic Design?

We've all become accustomed to seeing images on web pages. Should you just insert lots of images and consider your web page complete? Probably not. When it comes to images and colors, remember that often, less is more.

The use of images depends on many things:

• Whether the images add value to the page or just take up space—You want any images to support the text, not distract the reader from the original intent of the page.

• The size of the image relative to the rest of the page—If an image is large, the reader might spend too much time scrolling to see the text. Too many images

Click list
arrow to
change
location

Contents of
your folder
may differ

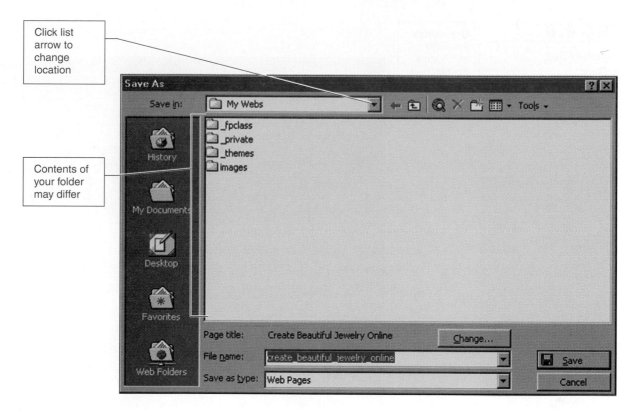

FIGURE 4.7

Save As Dialog Box

can be problematic to readers with slow Internet connections, requiring a lot of download time.

- The colors used in the images—Outrageous colors can be annoying. A loud color can become bothersome in short order. Garish colors fall in the same category as offensive language, and this is something you want to avoid.

Using a table to place a graphic image is a good way to insert an image in a controlled location. You can eliminate the appearance of the border and your reader will never know the table is there.

Steps

1. Click the **Preview** tab. The text appears in the table cell. Using a table is a good way of aligning and organizing text, but the table would look better without the border.

2. Click the **Normal** tab, click **Table** on the menu bar, point to **Properties,** then click **Table.** The Table Properties dialog box opens. You can turn the border off by changing the border size to zero.

3. Double-click the **Size** text box, type **0,** as shown in Figure 4.8, then click **OK.** The dialog box closes, and the table now displays a dotted border.

4. Click the **Preview** tab. The text appears in the table cell, but the table border is now invisible, as seen in Figure 4.9.

5. Click the **Normal** tab, confirm that the pointer is in the top left cell, then click **Insert Picture From File** on the Standard toolbar. The Select File dialog box opens.

FIGURE 4.8

Table Properties
Dialog Box

Determines
the width
of the table
border

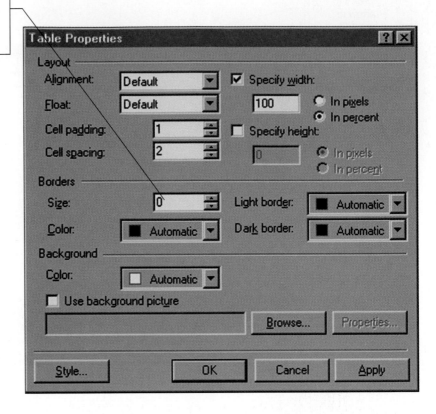

FIGURE 4.9

Invisible Table Border

FIGURE 4.10

Select File Dialog Box

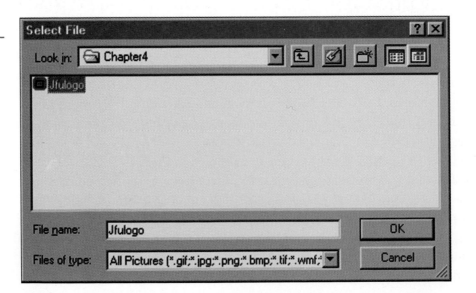

Cell expands to accommodate the image

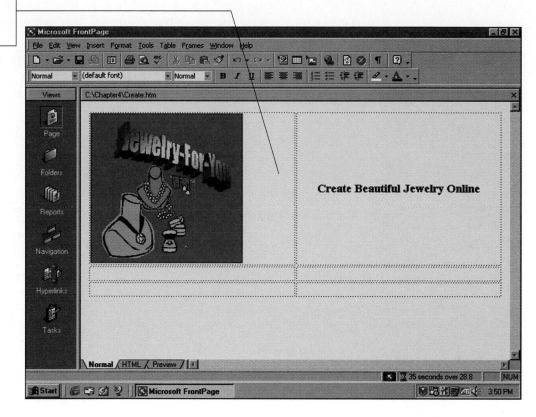

FIGURE 4.11

Graphic Image in Table

6. Click the **Look in** list arrow, locate your project files, select **Jfulogo,** as shown in Figure 4.10, then click **OK.** The image appears in the table in the top left cell. Compare your work to Figure 4.11.

7. Click the **Save** button 💾.

How Can I Use Color?

Color is an important part of any web page, and the effective use of color can have a great impact on your audience. Before you start working with website colors think about what you like to see when you visit a site. Do you like loud, outrageous colors? Perhaps there are occasions when these are suitable. But like graphic images, you probably don't want a background color to compete with your content. Think of the background of a web page like a wall in your home. For most people, the wall color is the backdrop for interesting items they choose to display.

In FrontPage, there are two ways to control the background color. You can change the color, or you can apply a theme. A **theme** is a series of coordinated colors that can be applied to many commonly found web page elements. Applying a theme is a kind of one-stop shopping: rather than individually changing the properties of web page elements, you can apply a theme and all the elements will be changed. You can easily change the background color of a web page.

Steps

1. Click **Format** on the menu bar, then click **Background.** The Page Properties dialog box opens, as seen in Figure 4.12.

2. Verify that the Background tab is active, then click the **Background** list arrow. A color palette displays. You can choose any color on the palette, or click More Colors to see additional choices.

3. Click the second box from the left in the second row of colors (the lime colored box), then click **OK.** Lime green appears in the background of the page, as shown in Figure 4.13. If you decide this is not a suitable color background for your web page, you can undo this color application using a button on the toolbar.

4. Click the **Undo** button ↶ on the Standard toolbar. The background returns to its previous color. You can apply a theme using the Format menu or by right-clicking anywhere on the background.

5. Right-click any background location, then click **Theme** on the pop-up menu. The Themes dialog box opens. A wide variety of themes are supplied with FrontPage.

6. Click **Arcs,** select only the Background picture checkbox as shown in Figure 4.14, then click **OK.** The theme is applied to the page, as shown in Figure 4.15.

7. Click the **Save** button, 💾 then click **OK** in the Save Embedded Files dialog box.

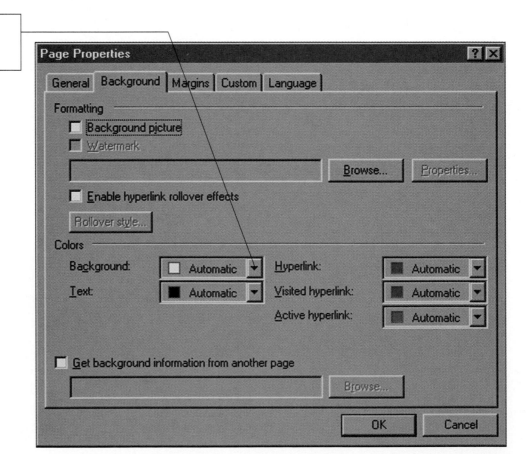

FIGURE 4.12

Page Properties Dialog Box

FIGURE 4.13
New Background Color

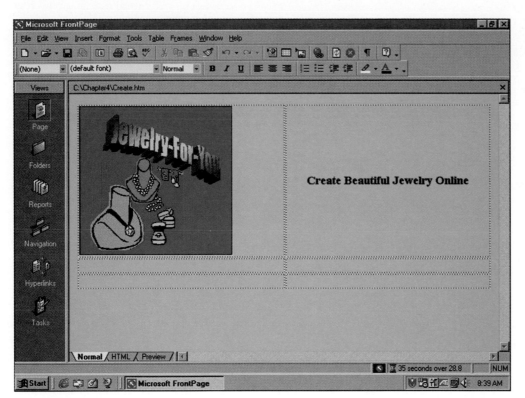

FIGURE 4.14
Themes Dialog Box

Available themes

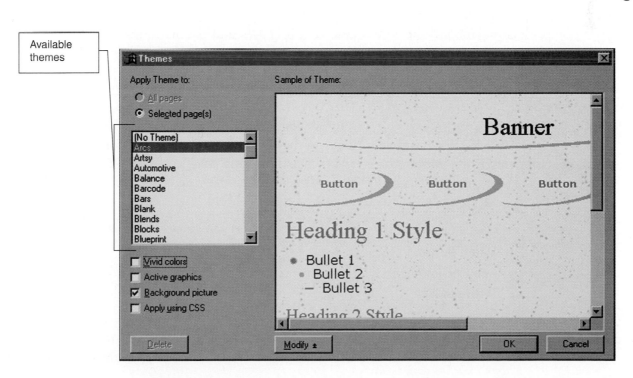

FIGURE 4.15

Theme Applied to
Page

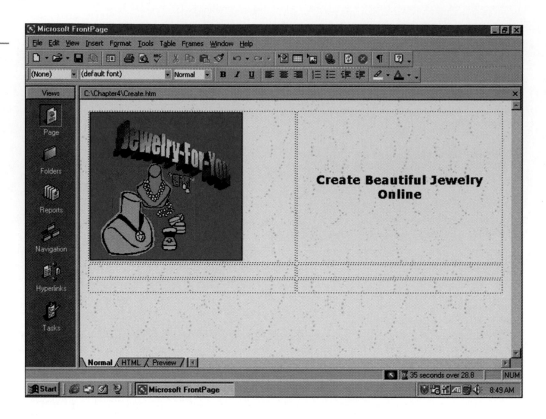

How Should I Design a Form?

The primary task of your eBusiness is to sell your products or services. In addition, each time someone visits your website or makes a purchase, you have the opportunity to collect important information.

The information you collect and analyze, a process called **data mining,** can be used to improve each customer's subsequent visits. The website in Figure 4.16 "remembers" the reader and her purchases and is able to make new purchase suggestions.

E-tip
As you know from your own experience, if a form looks disorganized or too long, you probably won't bother completing it. Remember this when you design your own forms.

What Elements Can I Include in a Form?

There are many data collection tools you can include in a form. There are two reasons to use these collection tools: to make form completion easy for your readers, and to make the data easy to analyze. Such collection devices include the following elements:

- Text box
- Check box
- Radio button
- Drop-down menu
- Push button

E-tip
You can include all these elements in a form, but that doesn't mean you should. Use of too many elements can make a form look cluttered and complicated.

Figure 4.17 contains sample elements. The page in Figure 4.18 contains a form with several elements: text boxes, option buttons, and push buttons. The alignment of the fields gives the form an easy-to-read ordered appearance.

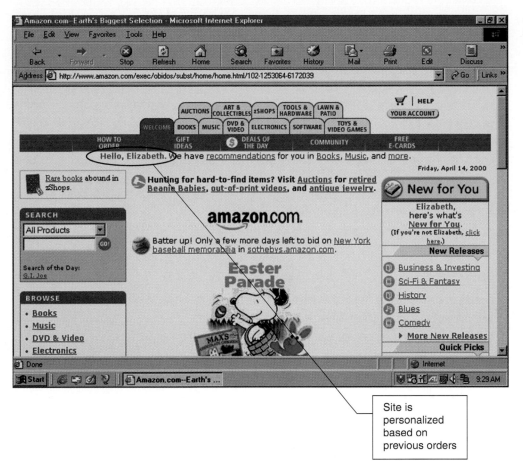

Site is
personalized
based on
previous orders

FIGURE 4.16

Data Mining in Action

Source: AMAZON.COM is a registered trademark of Amazon.com, Inc.

FIGURE 4.17

Form Element Samples

FIGURE 4.18

Online Form for Data
Collection

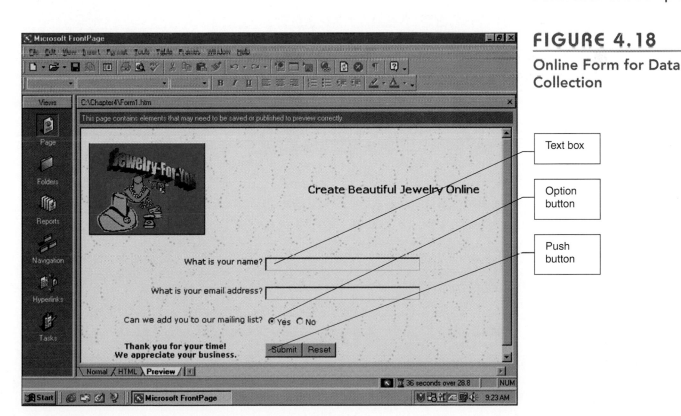

Text box

Option
button

Push
button

How Can I Create a Website for My Business?

Many programs can be used to create and modify web pages, but a website consists of more than one page, and linking the pages together can sometimes be tricky. Programs such as Microsoft FrontPage and Microsoft Publisher make it easy to create websites for a business. While each of these programs has different strengths and functions differently, they both contain helpful devices that make creating a website simple. Both programs make a wizard available to construct the site. A **wizard** is a series of dialog boxes containing specific questions. When the questions are complete, so is the task.

How Can I Create a Website Using FrontPage?

FrontPage contains wizards to help you build a variety of sites, including a Corporate Presence. Use the following steps to create a Corporate Presence website.

Steps

1. Click **File** on the menu bar, point to New, then click **Web.** The New dialog box opens, as seen in Figure 4.19.
2. Click the **Corporate Presence Wizard,** verify the location for the new web, then click **OK.** Folders are set up to accommodate the new website. A new pane displaying folders and files appears to the left of the page window.
3. Create necessary pages for the website.
4. Use the Navigation button to define relationships among the pages in the website.

FIGURE 4.19

New Dialog Box in FrontPage

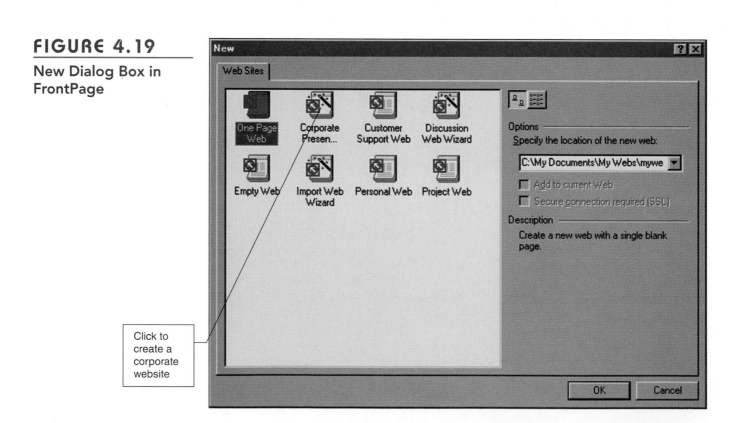

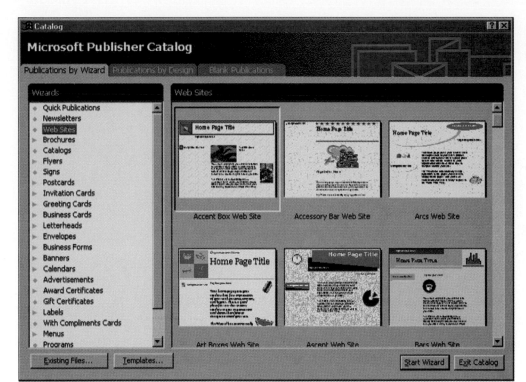

FIGURE 4.20

Publisher Catalog

How Can I Create a Website Using Publisher?

Publisher is a desktop publishing program that also contains website assistance. This program is oriented more toward manipulating graphic images and text. Use the following steps to create a website using Microsoft Publisher.

Steps

1. If the Catalog is not already open, click **File** on the menu bar, click **New,** then click **Web Sites.** The Catalog opens, as seen in Figure 4.20.

2. Click a site from the list, then click **Start Wizard.** A series of questions are displayed in the left-side windowpane.

3. Click **Next** after supplying answers in each window pane, then click **Finish.** The completed website will display in the workspace.

Where Can I Find Web Design Resources?

You can use your favorite search engine to find many design resources on the Web. Of course, these resources are constantly changing, but there are many from which to choose. Most of the resources contain examples and tutorials.

Steps

1. Connect to the Internet, open your browser, then go to your favorite search engine.

2. Type **design resources** in the search text box. The search engine displays the results, as shown in Figure 4.21.

FIGURE 4.21

Search Engine Results

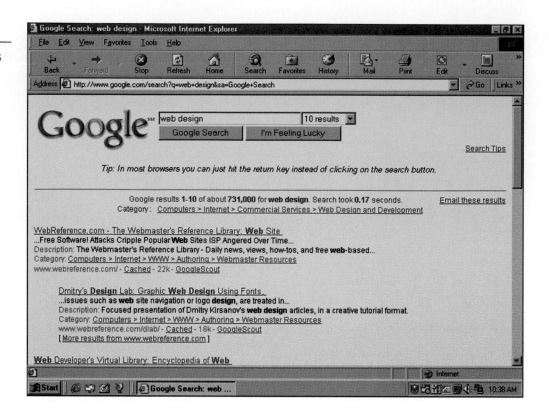

An excellent source of web page design tips is the Yale Style Manual. This site, shown in Figure 4.22, contains excellent descriptions and examples of good designs.

What Should I Consider for Special-Needs Audiences?

In addition to considering that every browser cannot successfully read each element in every web page, you also should consider the needs of your audience. Our world is a melting pot in which we all have different capabilities and limitations, and it is these potential deficiencies that should be addressed.

What Special Needs Exist?

Many web users have special needs: physical and mental disabilities that might make using your website difficult or impossible. These possibilities should be considered when designing a web page.

Users with color blindness may not be able to distinguish some colors used in your web pages. Visually impaired users who need larger type may not be able to read your text. Certain conditions make framed pages and blinking elements confusing and distracting and make focusing difficult.

It would be very difficult to create a website that accommodates the specific needs of every person. Consider the nature of the audience you are seeking, and be aware that certain design elements may cause difficulties. Some sites, such as the one shown in Figure 4.23, detail various types of disabilities and what you can do to make your site more accessible.

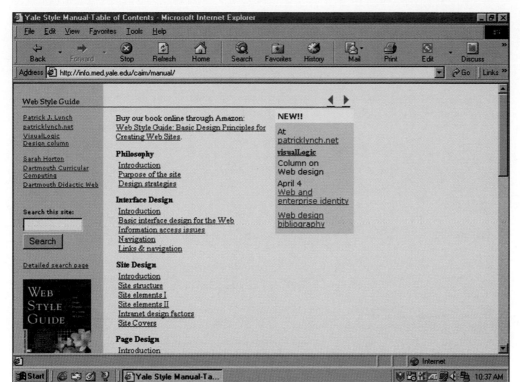

FIGURE 4.22

Yale Style Manual

Source: Copyright Lynch & Horton, 1997.

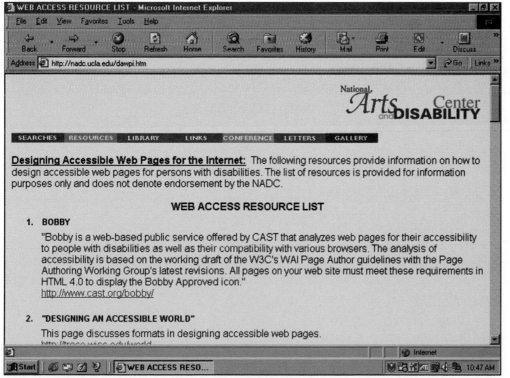

FIGURE 4.23

Special-Needs Design Tips

Source: Courtesy of the National Arts and Disability Center.

Checkpoint

Designing a web page takes more than the knowledge necessary to click the right toolbar buttons. A lot of thought is required when determining use of color, placement of graphic images, and form construction.

Many resources exist—most of them on the Web—that can be used to help you design the perfect site. You need to determine the nature of your audience and what features are necessary to make your site most efficient.

Keys

white space	attributes	default
navigation bar	alignment	theme
resolution	Standard toolbar	data mining
formatting	Formatting toolbar	wizard
font		

Milestones

Complete the following statements:

1. Areas on a page containing no text or graphics are called _____ _____.
2. A lower _____ displays text and images larger but shows less information on the screen.
3. Adding boldface to text is an example of applying an _____.
4. Font and font size buttons are generally located on the _____ toolbar.
5. The _____ tab is the default setting in FrontPage.
6. You can change text alignment using buttons on the _____ toolbar.
7. The Save button is located on the _____ toolbar.
8. Undo an action using a button on the _____ toolbar.
9. _____ is the process of collecting and analyzing customer information.
10. In a form, you can type characters in a _____ _____.

Complete the following exercises:

1. Locate several design resources on the Web, noting their URLs. Which of these sources do you like? Why?
2. Given the different possible screen resolutions, which resolution should you use when designing a web page? Why?

Your Turn

Your Shoes-By-Mail eBusiness is almost ready to begin. All you need is a preliminary web page design. Make a preliminary sketch of what you would like to see in the initial page of this website.

CHAPTER 5

creating a site

How Do I Create a Website?

Once you have decided to take the website plunge, and have sketched out the design, it's time to actually create the site. You want your website to look like a professional created it—elegant and simple to use.

Although this is a challenging exercise, it is not nearly as traumatic as it once was. A few years ago, creating web pages required the use of complicated codes. Now, you can create a site using commonly available software programs that require little coding knowledge.

Kim has decided to try her hand at creating the website, although she has never done anything like this before. She has Microsoft FrontPage on her computer, and has made a few practice runs before attempting to create the Jewelry-For-You site. So far, the wizards and help screens have left her feeling that she can actually complete this task.

Creating a Website

CHAPTER OUTLINE

How Do I Plan a Website?

How Can I Find Web-Authoring Tools?

What Is HTML?

How Is a Website Created?

How Can I Modify a Web Page?

How Do I Add a List to a Page?

How Can I Add a Hover Button?

How Can I Create a Navigation Bar?

FIGURE 5.1

eBusiness Website

How Do I Plan a Website?

Make real notes in addition to mental notes. Keep track of websites containing positive and negative features.

By this time, you've been looking at a lot of websites. You've probably seen features you really like, as well as those you find irritating. Make mental notes of both types of features; you probably don't want to duplicate something you yourself don't like.

How Does a Web Page Differ from a Website?

What's the difference between a web page and a website? A **web page** is a single page, while a **website** is a collection of related—and linked—pages. A website can contain an infinite number of web pages, and in most cases, the pages in a website contain a common design theme that links them visually.

What Should I Be Thinking as I'm Planning My Website?

When you're planning a website for your eBusiness, you should be thinking of your customers' comfort, as well as increasing sales. After all, if your customers don't like your website, they probably won't be using it.

Several principles should be uppermost in your mind as you plan your website:

- **Make a sketch.** Actually draw the pages you think you'll need. Each sketch doesn't have to be highly artistic, just containing enough information to help you envision what features you'd like and where you'd like to see them. Figure 5.2 shows a preliminary sketch of the Jewelry-For-You website. Think about how customers will be using your website: what pages they'll be jumping between and what other information they might be interested in.

- **Simple, yet elegant.** Your business website is there to conduct commerce, not to dazzle readers with your design abilities. Use tasteful colors, no more than two fonts per page (in legible sizes), and simple graphics that add value without draining computer resources.

- **Add value.** While the primary goal of your business website is to sell products or services, be on the lookout for information that might be of interest to your customers.

Start early collecting URLs for interesting sites that you can add to an additional page.

How Can I Find Web-Authoring Tools?

Web-authoring tools, sometimes called *web editors,* are programs that make it possible to create web pages and websites. Depending on the computer you have, you may already have one or more programs with web-authoring capabilities. If not, you can easily find such programs using the Internet as a resource.

Examples of specifically designed web-authoring tools are

- Adobe PageMill
- Adobe SiteMill
- Claris Home Page
- Hot Dog Pro

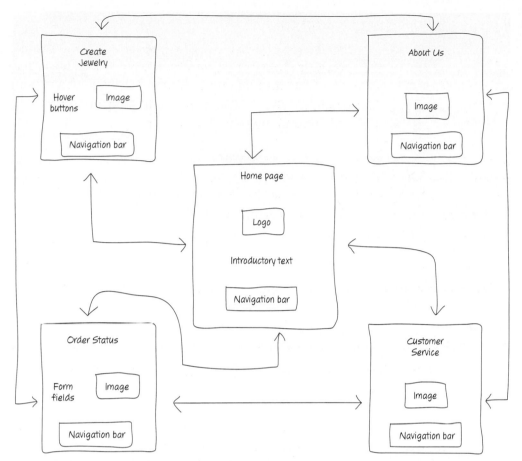

FIGURE 5.2

Preliminary Website Sketch

- HotMetal Pro
- Microsoft FrontPage

Other programs have multiple uses and have limited web-authoring capabilities, such as

- Corel NetPerfect
- Lotus FastSite
- Microsoft Publisher
- Microsoft Word

What Tools Are out There?

Establish an Internet connection, open your browser, then open your favorite search engine. You can use any search engine to locate web-authoring tools. Figures 5.3 and 5.4 show results of searches using two different search engines. Notice that both search engines returned different results.

 You should use multiple engines to locate as many resources as possible.

Figures 5.5 and 5.6 display some of the additional resources you can find using the Web. You may find coverage choppy and inconsistent from one site to another. By visiting a variety of sites, you'll increase your knowledge tremendously and be able to form your own opinions.

FIGURE 5.3

Google Search Results

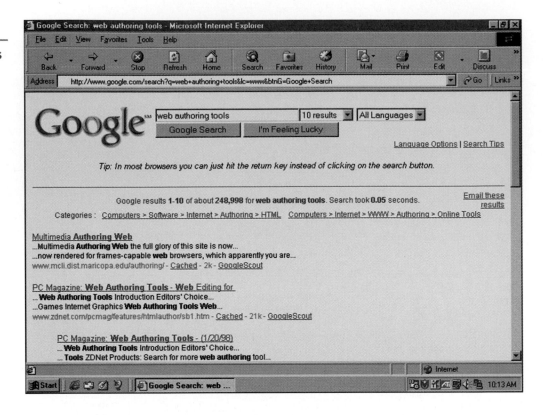

FIGURE 5.4

Go.com Search Results

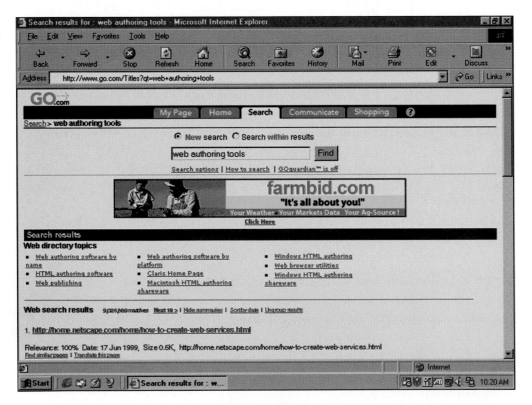

Source: Reprinted by permission. Infoseek, Ultrasmart, Ultraseek, Ultraseek Server, Infoseek Desktop, Infoseek Ultra, ISeek, Quickseek, Imageseek, Ultrashop, and the Infoseek logos are trademarks of Infoseek Corporation which may be registered in certain jurisdictions. Other trademarks shown are trademarks of their respective owners. Copyright © 1998-2000 Infoseek Corporation. All rights reserved.

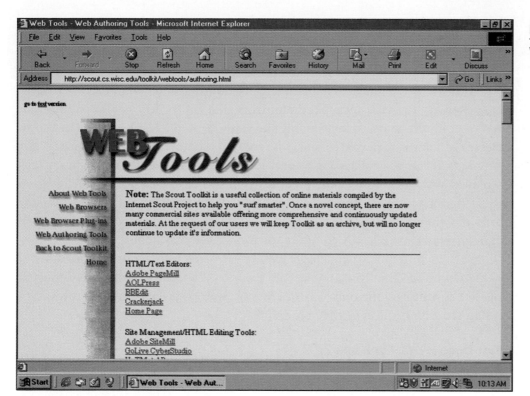

FIGURE 5.5

Web Tools

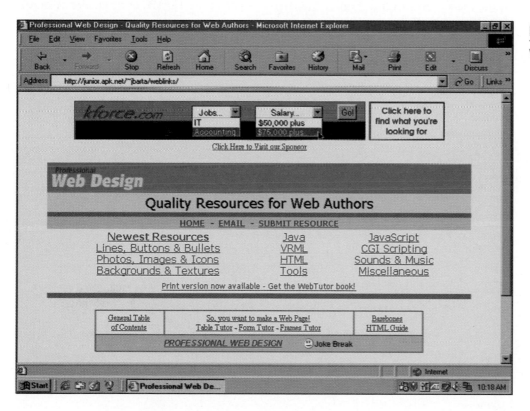

FIGURE 5.6

Web Design Resources

What Is HTML?

Regardless of the web-authoring tools you use, all web pages—and sites—have one thing in common. They are made up of HTML codes. **HTML** stands for HyperText Markup Language. This language is nothing more than a collection of codes, or **tags,** inserted into text documents that make it possible for different types of computers to display roughly the same content. Each tag tells the computer on which it's displayed to make the content have certain characteristics. For example, text can be displayed in a specific size due to its tags. In many cases, tags are placed at the beginning and end of text. (In some cases, a tag may be inserted only at the beginning of the text it defines. It is assumed that the next new tag "turns off" the initial tag.) Because of HTML, a page created using a Macintosh can be displayed on a UNIX computer as well as other systems.

Like other computer languages, HTML has evolved into a more complex set of tags than were originally available. And prior to the existence of web-authoring tools like FrontPage, the only way of creating web pages was to open a text editor, like WordPad, and type the tags and text.

What Does HTML Look Like?

As you look at Figure 5.7, you can see text with bracketed tags. These tags are the HTML instructions that tell each computer platform how to display a specific word, phrase, or image. This hodgepodge of text and tags is difficult to create and equally difficult to read. Figure 5.8 displays the same HTML code in FrontPage's HTML view. As you write a page in FrontPage, these codes are being created and are available for viewing by clicking the HTML tab.

FIGURE 5.7

HTML Code in
WordPad

Indicates a heading style

Creates a new paragraph

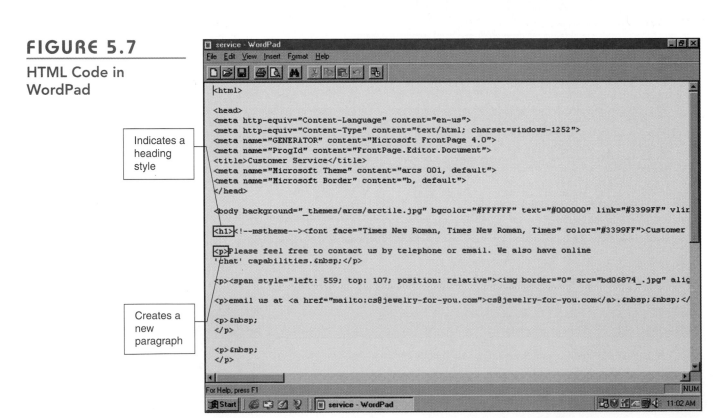

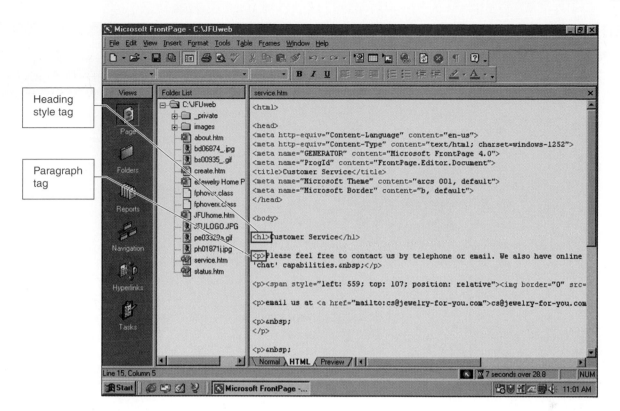

FIGURE 5.8

HTML Code in
FrontPage

In FrontPage, like many web-authoring programs, tags and text are displayed in different colors. This makes reading the code much easier than wading through endless lines of identical-looking words. Figure 5.9 displays the same web page in a browser.

How Is a Website Created?

The advantage to using a program such as Microsoft FrontPage to create a website is that much of what you need is automated. Rather than spending time learning the nuances of writing HTML code, you can put what little time you have to good use creating your site.

Each software program uses its own nomenclature, and FrontPage is no exception. FrontPage refers to the initial home page, all the pages associated with it, as well as graphic images, multimedia files, and any other files that support a site's functionality as a **web.**

When you open FrontPage using the Programs menu, a blank web page automatically opens. You can use the blank page to design a single web page, but because you are going to be designing a series of interconnected pages, you need to use a slightly different approach when creating a website.

You can use FrontPage to create a web by answering questions in a series of dialog boxes.

E-tip: Because many files can be used in a website, it makes good administrative sense to store all the related files and folders within a single folder.

FIGURE 5.9

Web Page in Browser

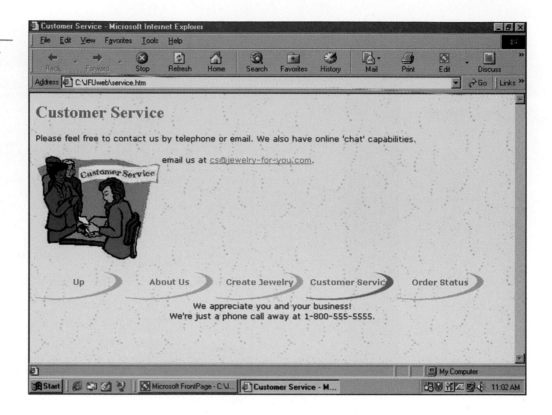

Steps

1. Click **Start** 🏁Start on the taskbar, point to **Programs,** then click **Microsoft FrontPage.** The FrontPage splash screen displays and a blank web page opens.

2. Click **File** on the menu bar, point to **New,** then click **Web.** The New dialog box opens. This dialog box contains templates you can use when creating a new web or page. A **template** is a predesigned page or web that contains fonts, colors, and patterns on which you can base your website. Templates are available in most programs to improve your efficiency.

3. Click the **Corporate Presence Wizard,** as shown in Figure 5.10, click the **Specify the location of the new web** list arrow, find the location approved for your web, click **OK,** click **Yes** if a warning box to convert a folder into a new web appears, then click **OK.**

   The Corporate Presence Web Wizard opens, as seen in Figure 5.11. You can accept the default selections by clicking Next.

4. Click **Next** 11 times (until the company name is requested), type **Jewelry-For-You** in the **What is the full name of your company?** text box, type **Jewelry** in the **What is the one-word version of this name?** text box, type **100 Main Street, NY, NY** in the **What is your company's street address?** text box, click **Next** twice, click **Choose Web Theme,** click **Arcs,** click **Active graphics,** click **Background picture,** click **OK,** click **Next,** deselect the **Show Task View** after web check box is uploaded, then click **Finish.**

   The Folder List displays showing all the folders and files created by the wizard. You can view any page by double-clicking the file in the Folder List.

5. Double-click **index.htm.** The Home page displays, as shown in Figure 5.12.

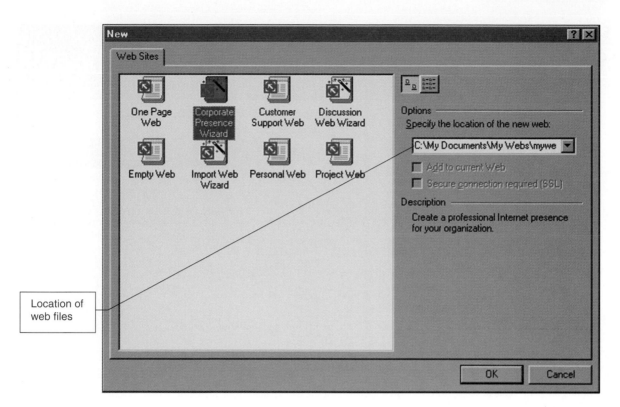

Location of
web files

FIGURE 5.10

New Dialog Box

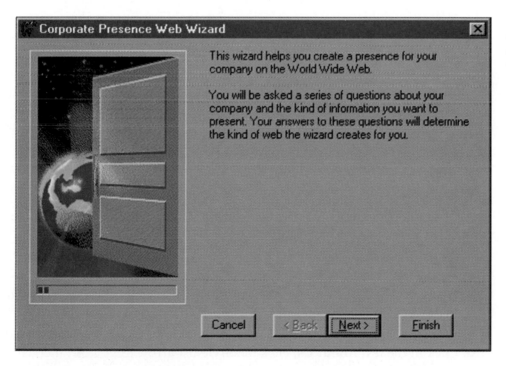

FIGURE 5.11

Corporate Presence
Web Wizard

FIGURE 5.12

Home Page Created
by Wizard

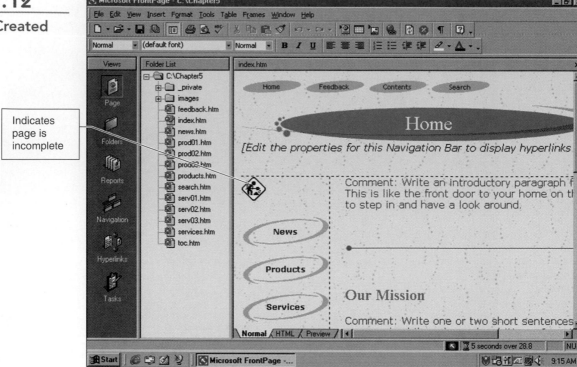

Indicates
page is
incomplete

How Can I Modify a Web Page?

The odds of designing and a creating the perfect web page are slim to none. No matter how much planning you do, you will probably want to make some modifications. Some of the types of changes you may want to make include adding and deleting text and changing the appearance of text.

Moving text on a web page is done in the same manner as in most word processors. You can select text, then cut and paste it elsewhere, or drag-and-drop it in a new location. As in word processing, a style can be applied to text to quickly change the formatting. A **style** is a preformatted collection of one or more attributes that can be applied to selected text. In HTML, a style is used to influence the appearance of text, as not all computers display attributes in the same manner.

Steps

1. Click the **Open button** list arrow 📂 ▾ on the Standard toolbar, click **Open Web,** locate the **JFUweb folder,** then click **Open.** The folders and files used in the web appear in the Folder List. You want to make changes to the file containing information about the company.

2. Double-click **About.htm** in the Folder List. The file displays, as shown in Figure 5.13. You can apply a style using a list arrow in the Formatting toolbar.

3. Click in the text **About Us,** click the **Style** list arrow (None) ▾ , then click **Heading 1.** Compare your text to Figure 5.14. The font, color, and font size were determined by the theme.

4. Click anywhere in the text Types of Jewelry, click (None) ▾ , then click **Heading 2.** The new heading displays in a smaller font. To preserve the original file, you can save this page using a different name.

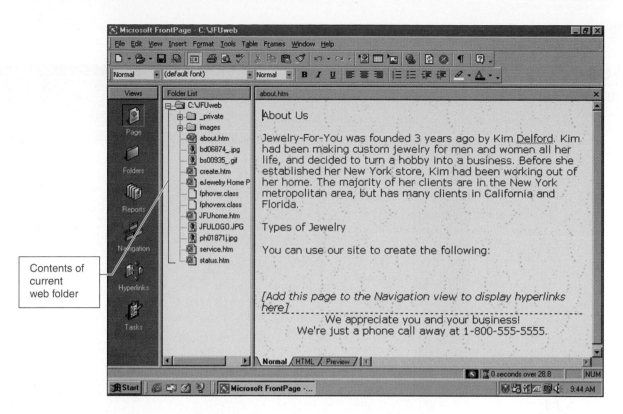

Contents of current web folder

FIGURE 5.13

Web Page and Folder List

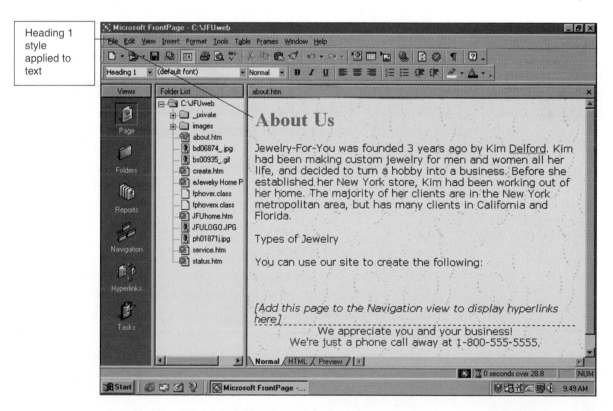

Heading 1 style applied to text

FIGURE 5.14

Style Applied to Text

97

FIGURE 5.15

Modified Page

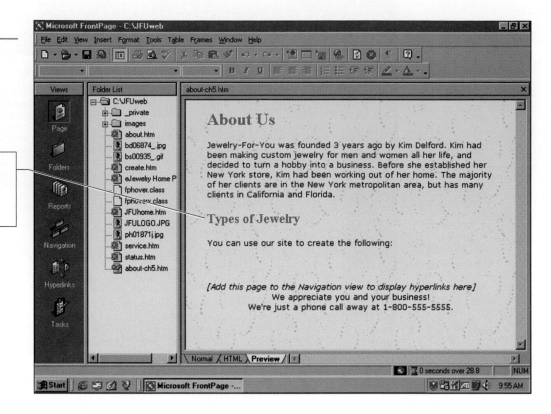

Heading 2 style is smaller than Heading 1

---

5. Click **File** on the menu bar, click Save As, type **about-ch5** in the File name text box, then click **Save.** The file is saved using the new name. You can see how the file will look using the Preview tab.

6. Click the **Preview** tab. Compare your file to Figure 5.15.

How Do I Add a List to a Page?

You may find it helpful to present web page information in a list format. Generally, lists are shown with preceding bullets or numbers. Bullets are used when any order can be used, whereas numbers are used when the order of the items is critical.

You can create a list using buttons on the Formatting toolbar, and you can use those buttons to alternate between numbered and bulleted lists.

Steps

1. Click the **Normal** tab. The view changes to Normal.

2. Click the line beneath **You can use our site to create the following:** You can create a numbered list using a button on the Formatting toolbar.

3. Click the **Numbering** button ![icon] on the Formatting toolbar. Once ![icon] is selected, a bullet will precede text that follows.

4. Type **Earrings,** press **Enter,** type **Necklaces,** press **Enter,** then type **Bracelets.** The text appears as numbered items, as shown in Figure 5.16. Numbered lists are generally used to indicate that steps should be taken in a particular order. This list would be better suited as a bulleted list.

 Items in a numbered list will automatically be renumbered if text is moved.

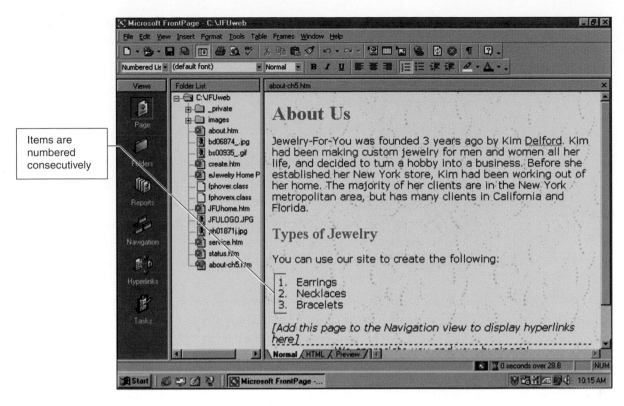

Items are numbered consecutively

FIGURE 5.16
Numbered List

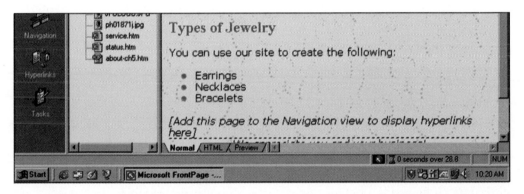

FIGURE 5.17
Bulleted List

5. Select the three numbered items, click the **Bullets** button 📇 on the Formatting toolbar, then click anywhere on the page to deselect the text. The numbers have changed to bullets, as shown in Figure 5.17.
6. Click the **Save** button 💾 on the Standard toolbar.

How Can I Add a Hover Button?

Special effects, such as hover buttons, can be added to a web page. A **hover button** is an object that changes its appearance when the mouse pointer is held over the button face. An **object** is any item placed on a page that is surrounded by **handles**—small squares in each corner—when it is selected. You can control the properties of a hover button, including the text displayed on its face; the color of the button, both before and after the hover effect; and the specific hover effect. Once you have applied hover button properties, you can see the results in the Preview tab.

Steps

1. Double-click **Create.htm** in the Folder List. The page displays, as shown in Figure 5.18. Four hover buttons have already been placed on this page. You want to add an additional hover button that puts all the selected pieces together.

2. Click the line beneath the **Findings** button, click **Insert** on the menu bar, point to **Component,** then click **Hover Button.** The Hover Button Properties dialog box opens, as shown in Figure 5.19.

3. Type **Assemble** in the Button text textbox, click the **Button color** list arrow, click **Aqua** (the third color box from the left in the second row of standard colors), then click the **Font** button. The Font dialog box opens, as shown in Figure 5.20.

4. Click the **Color** list arrow, click **Automatic,** click **OK.** When the pointer is placed over the button, a different visual effect occurs. You can change the effect of the hover button using the Effect list arrow.

5. Click the **Effect** list arrow, click **Bevel Out,** then click **OK.** This button will have a different appearance than the other buttons on this page. You can save this page using a different name to preserve the original file.

6. Click **File** on the menu bar, click **Save As,** type **create-ch5** in the File name text box, then click **Save.** You can view the button using the Preview tab.

7. Click the **Preview** tab, then move the pointer over each of the buttons. Figure 5.21 shows the effect of the new button when the pointer is held over it.

FIGURE 5.18

Page with Hover Buttons

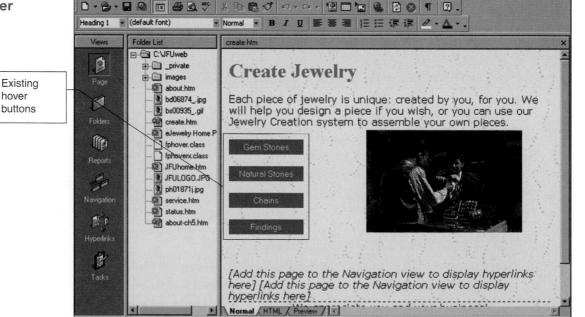

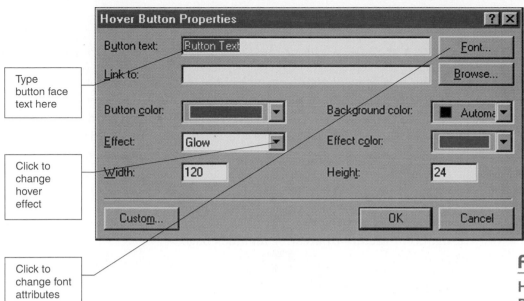

Type button face text here

Click to change hover effect

Click to change font attributes

FIGURE 5.19

Hover Button Properties Dialog Box

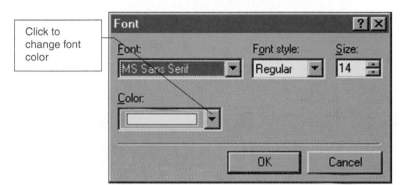

Click to change font color

FIGURE 5.20

Font Dialog Box

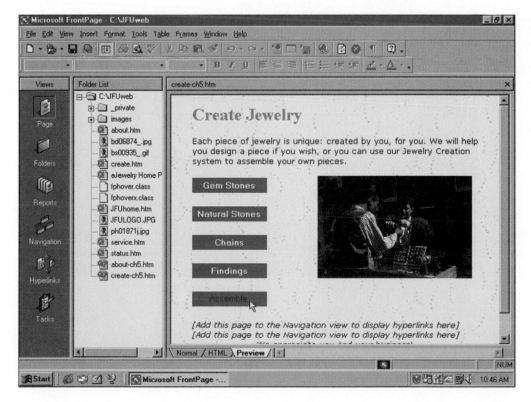

FIGURE 5.21

New Hover Button Added

How Can I Create a Navigation Bar?

It is important that users of your website be able to jump easily from one page to another. To do this, you need to define the structure of the site. Then you can create a navigation bar to make it easy to find each page. A **navigation bar** usually contains one button for each page in the site; it can be located at the top, bottom, left edge, or right edge of a page. If you have applied a theme to your website, it will be used in the navigation bar.

Steps

1. Click **View** on the menu bar, then click **Navigation.** You can create a navigation structure by creating an index page.

2. Click the **New Page** button 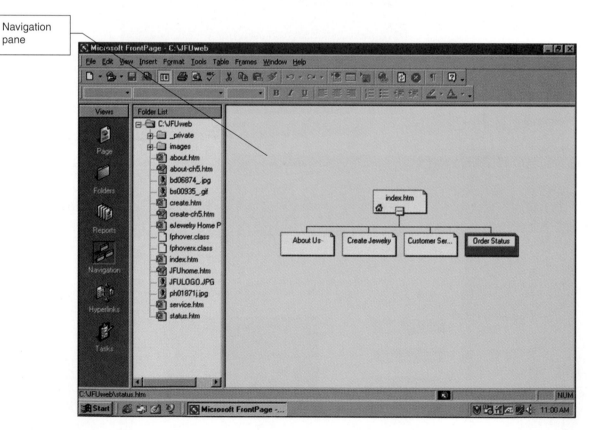 on the Standard toolbar. An index page is created. You create the structure by dragging file names to the index. This creates a hierarchical structure, as you would find in an organizational chart.

3. Click **about-ch5.htm** from the Folder List, then drag it beneath **index.htm.** The file title appears in the blue navigation pane.

FIGURE 5.22

Navigation Relationship Structure

4. Repeat step 3 using **create-ch5.htm, service.htm,** and **status.htm,** using Figure 5.22 as a guide. The titles for all four pages appear in the navigation pane.

5. Click **Format** on the menu bar, then click **Shared Borders.** The Shared Borders dialog box opens. The shared border will contain the navigation bar. You want the navigation bar to display at the bottom of all the pages.

6. Click the **All pages** option button, select the **Bottom** check box, then click **OK.** The default shared border text can be selected and the navigation bar inserted.

7. Click the **shared border** text, click **Insert** on the menu bar, then click **Navigation Bar.** The Navigation Bar Properties dialog box opens, as shown in Figure 5.23. The relationship between the four pages and the home page is that of children to parent.

8. Click the **Child level** option button, the **Home page** check box, then click **OK.** You can view the navigation bar in any of the child pages.

9. Double-click **create-ch5.htm** in the Folder List. If necessary, scroll up to view the navigation bar shown in Figure 5.24.

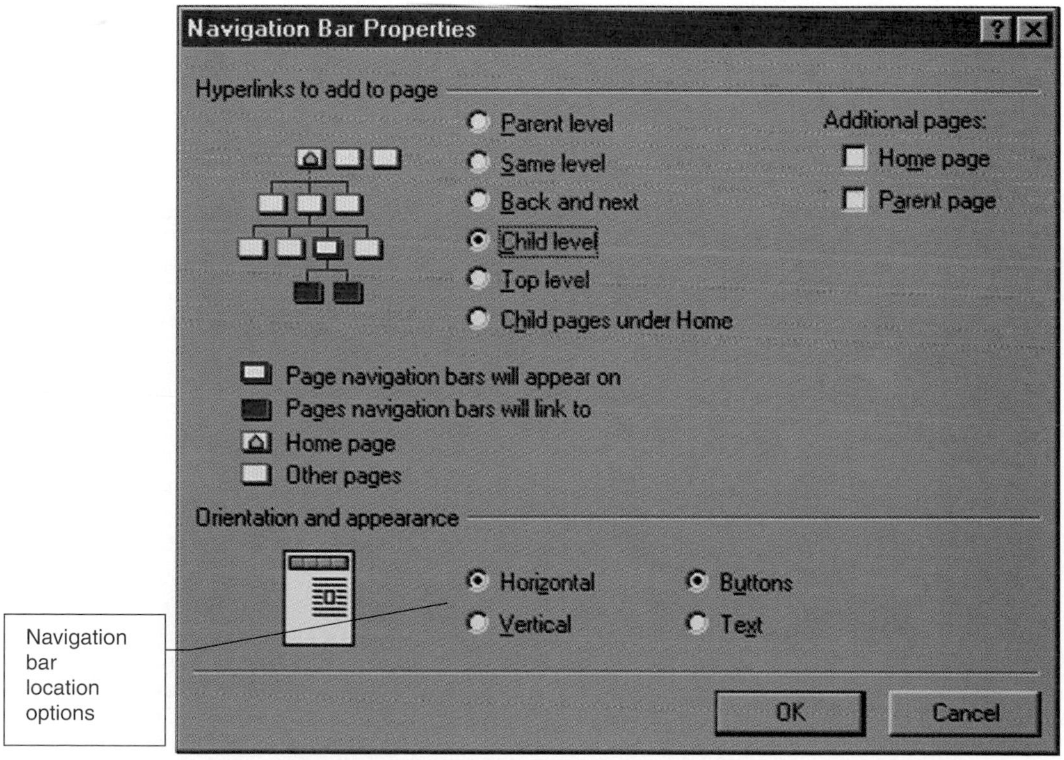

FIGURE 5.23

Navigation Bar
Properties Dialog Box

FIGURE 5.24

Navigation Bar in Web
Page

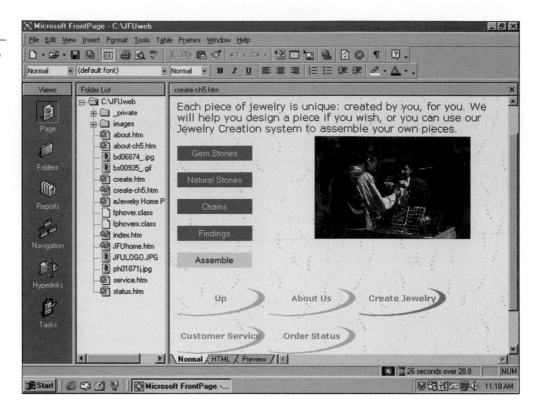

Checkpoint

Designing a web page takes more than the knowledge necessary to click the right tool-bar buttons. A lot of thought is required when determining use of color, placement of graphic images, and form construction.

Many resources exist—most of them on the Web—that can be used to help you design the perfect site. You need to determine the nature of your audience and what features are necessary to make your site most efficient.

Keys

web page	tags	hover button
website	web	object
web-authoring tools	template	handles
HTML	style	navigation bar

Milestones

Complete the following statements:

1. A web _____ is a collection of related, linked pages.
2. Web-authoring tools are also called web _____.
3. HTML stands for _____ _____ Language.
4. HTML codes are called _____.
5. You can create a web page using a(n) _____, a predesigned page that contains fonts, colors, and patterns.
6. A preformatted collection of font attributes is called a(n) _____.
7. The Style list arrow is located on the _____ toolbar.
8. Use a _____ list when the order of items is critical.

9. Small squares that appear when an object is selected are called _____.

10. A guide that helps users jump to other pages in your website is called a(n) _____ _____.

Complete the following exercises:

1. Locate and print the home pages of five corporate websites that use a navigation bar. Where on the page are these tools located? What do you think is the best location for a navigational tool?

2. Use your favorite search engine to locate different web-authoring tools. What features are commonly available in these programs? What unique features have you found? Use your favorite word processor to describe your findings.

Make up a fictitious eBusiness, then use the FrontPage web wizard to create a corporate website. Fill in as much information as you can on the home page, then save and print the page.

CHAPTER 6

Developing

How Can I Enhance a Web Page?

So, you've created your website, but now you want to add features such as graphic images and hyperlinks that make your pages unique. Graphic images do more than just take up space; they say in an instant what you might need paragraphs to say. In a product-oriented eBusiness, you can use images of your products to enhance the site.

Using FrontPage, it is easy to add images. You can add links throughout your pages to make it simple for site visitors to jump to other related websites. Forms can be used to collect data from your site visitors. The data you collect can be helpful in your continuing marketing efforts and can help you improve your site.

Now that the Jewelry-For-You site has been created, Kim can spend some time making modifications that will enhance the site. It's already a good site: she just wants it to be better.

Enhancing a Web Page

CHAPTER OUTLINE

What Is a Graphic Image?

Where Can I Get Images?

How Can I Insert an Image?

How Is a Hyperlink Inserted?

How Are Multimedia Files Used?

What Is a Form?

How Is a Form Created?

How Can I Modify a Form?

FIGURE 6.1

Working on
Enhancements

What Is a Graphic Image?

In a web page, a **graphic image** is a picture in an electronic format. You get graphic images in your computer by purchasing them (and then accessing them using a diskette or CD-ROM) or using some other external source. When you place an image in a web page, your web editor creates HTML codes that tell the page the exact location and description of the file. Figure 6.2 shows a website that uses graphic images and text as links to other pages.

 Most scanners operate in a similar manner. Digital cameras vary from brand to brand in the way images are downloaded.

A scanner or digital camera is an example of an external image source. A **scanner** lets you take a print image, such as an advertisement or photograph, and convert it into an electronic file. A **digital camera** takes photographs in the same fashion as a film camera, except that instead of film, it uses some form of memory card. Images are recorded on the (reusable) memory device and then uploaded to your computer. There are so many digital cameras that it can be hard to choose. Figure 6.3 contains a website that helps you determine the right digital camera for your needs.

Graphic images tend to be much larger than text files. You want web pages to be small to make downloading faster and easier. The problem of wanting to use large images in an environment that demands small size necessitated the development of electronic file formats that reduce image sizes. Table 6.1 lists some commonly available graphic image formats.

Which Format Should I Use?

How can you decide which file format to use? Sometimes you don't have a choice. When you purchase artwork, sometimes called **clipart,** it is already in a particu-

FIGURE 6.2

Images and Text Used as Links

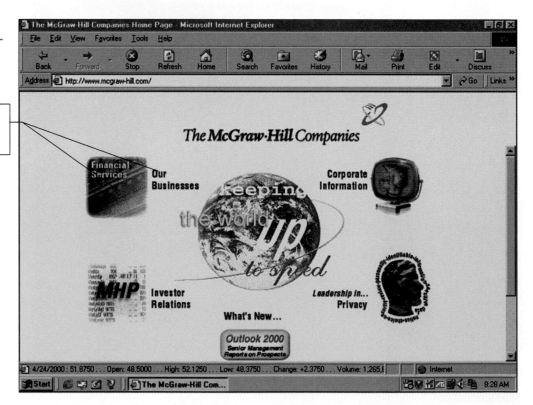

Click the image or the text

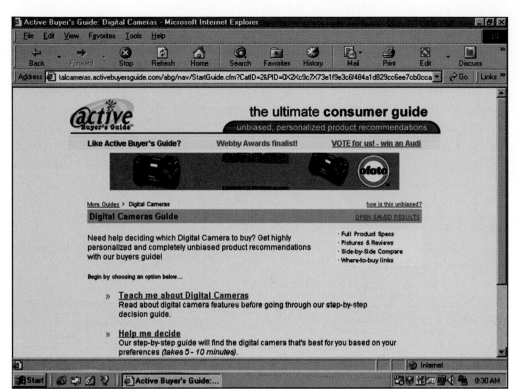

FIGURE 6.3

Website Helps You
Choose a Digital
Camera

Format	Extension
Graphics Interchange Format	GIF
Joint Photographic Experts Group	JPEG, JPG
Windows Bitmap	BMP
Tagged Image File Format	TIFF
PC Paintbrush	PCX
Windows Meta File	WMF

TABLE 6.1

Commonly Used
Graphic Image
Formats

lar format that is probably just fine. Some file formats slightly alter the appearance of an image, making colors appear muddier or images blurrier. Some formats reduce file size by compressing the image. In the compression process, some data is discarded. Such a format is referred to as **lossy.** The net result is a smaller image file. Unfortunately, the image may lose some clarity. The lossy GIF format compresses files while maintaining good image quality. The JPEG format supports 24-bit color, whereas the GIF format supports 8-bit color.

In most cases, this is not a huge problem. Web images must be small enough to make transmission smooth but large enough to get the point across.

Are There Other Considerations?

Although most browsers can support graphic images, not all do. In addition, not everyone has a fast Internet connection, so some users may prefer to view your page without images. For these reasons, you should offer a text-only version of your pages and include text descriptions of images.

Where Can I Get Images?

Many programs come with their own collection of images. But it seems that no matter how much artwork you have, you always seem to need, or want, more. You can find many websites that offer free or low-cost images. Figure 6.4 shows the results of a web search that lists many graphic image sites.

The quality you need in an image can depend on your use. For example, if you are putting together a corporate brochure that will be commercially printed, you'll probably want to use a professional-grade image. These images tend to be larger in file size and larger in price.

What Kind of Image Topics Are Available?

Graphic images are available on virtually any topic. A site featuring music-related graphic images is shown in Figure 6.5. There are also sites that can create electronic files for you, as shown in Figure 6.6.

As you become more familiar with graphic images, you'll be able to find specific sites that cater to your needs.

How Can I Insert an Image?

Once you have an image, you'll probably want to use it in your web page. In many cases, you'll probably put the text in your web page before adding a graphic image. Even though it's easier for people to recognize images rather than text, it seems that the design phase always begins by laying out words.

FIGURE 6.4

Search Engine Results

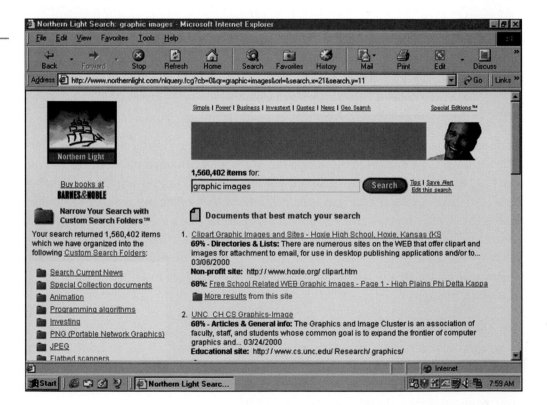

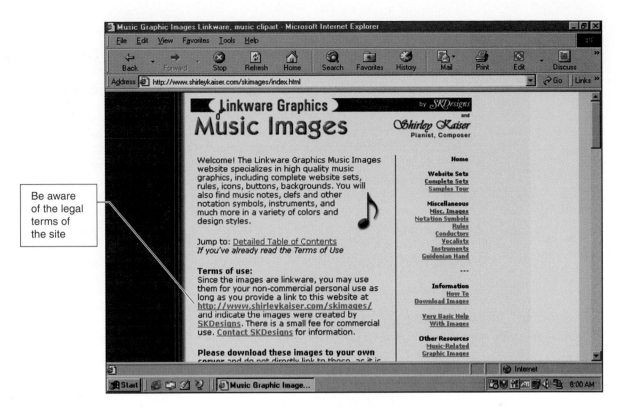

Be aware of the legal terms of the site

FIGURE 6.5

Music-Related Graphic Images

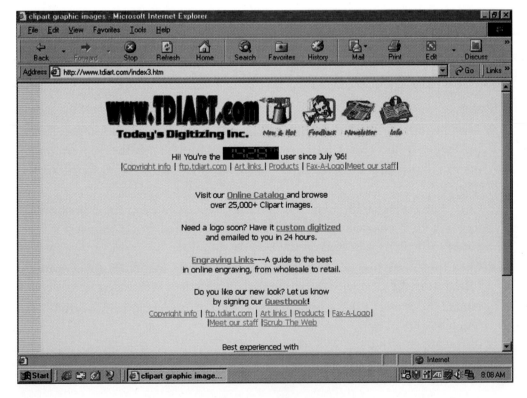

FIGURE 6.6

Commercial Clipart Site

ETHICS AND THE WEB

So much of what we find on the Web is free, that often it doesn't occur to us to ask for permission. When you think about it, anyone with a scanner and a website can create images in a digital format and post them on the Internet. Is this ethical? The proliferation of inexpensive scanners and digital cameras means that our images, information, and ideas are at risk.

The concept of **intellectual property**—knowledge, information, a logo, or a procedure, to name a few—is not new. Copyright laws and infringement issues have existed for years, but increased Internet use has added a new dimension to the question of ownership and piracy of intellectual property. Because it is so easy for any individual to obtain graphic images from books or websites and then use them in web pages, actual ownership is often not clear and it's difficult to police. Even as we speak, new ground is being broken, and new legislation is before the courts to determine what belongs to whom and how to protect and define ownership rights.

If your picture is taken with a digital camera and posted on a website without your permission, haven't your rights been violated? Common courtesy would dictate that your permission would be obtained before the image is posted, but this does not always occur. Since the Internet is largely unregulated, we are all on the honor system.

Can content control be exercised over website authors when the Internet itself is not monitored or regulated? Who should be responsible for preventing copyright infringement of intellectual property? It is difficult enough to control copyright infringement in the nondigital world; the ease of access within the digital arena makes such theft even more possible and that much harder to control.

While art that accompanies a program is often referred to as clipart, an electronic file that has been purchased, scanned, or uploaded is sometimes called a **picture file.** You can insert a picture file using a toolbar button.

Steps

1. Start FrontPage, click the **Open** button 🖿 on the Standard toolbar, locate the Project Files, click **Chapter6,** then click **Open.** The file Chapter6.htm opens. To preserve the original file, you can save the file using a different name.

2. Click **File** on the menu bar, click **Save As,** type **service** in the File name text box, then click **Save.** The file has been renamed. You can insert a picture file using a button on the Standard toolbar.

3. Click the empty line beneath Please, then click the **Insert Picture From File** button 🖼 on the Standard toolbar. The Select File dialog box opens.

4. Locate the Project Files using the Look in list arrow, click the file **bd06874_,** then click **OK.** The image appears in the web page as shown in Figure 6.7. You can modify the image

> **E-tip**
> The Pictures toolbar displays when an image is selected.

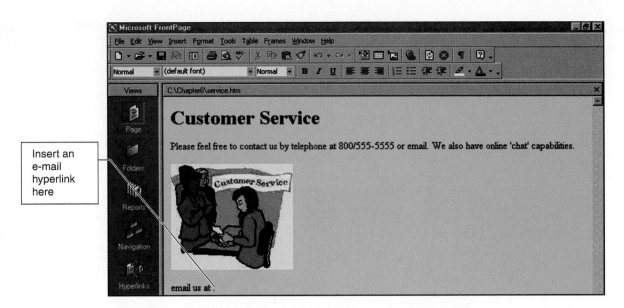

Insert an e-mail hyperlink here

FIGURE 6.7

Image in Web Page

TABLE 6.2

Commonly Used Pictures Toolbar Buttons

Name	Button	Name	Button
Text		More contrast	
Bring forward		Less contrast	
Send backward		More brightness	
Rotate left		Less brightness	
Rotate right		Crop	
Flip horizontal		Wash out	
Flip vertical		Restore	

using buttons on the Pictures toolbar. Some types of modifications you can do using buttons in the Pictures toolbar include flipping and rotating an image, cropping, and changing the contrast in an image. Table 6.2 displays some of the commonly used buttons in the Pictures toolbar.

5. Click the **image,** click the **Less Brightness** button on the Pictures toolbar twice. The white area in the image changes to a light gray color, as shown in Figure 6.8.

6. Click the **Save** button on the Standard toolbar, then click **OK** in the Save Embedded Files dialog box.

FIGURE 6.8

Modified Image

Selected image

Pictures toolbar

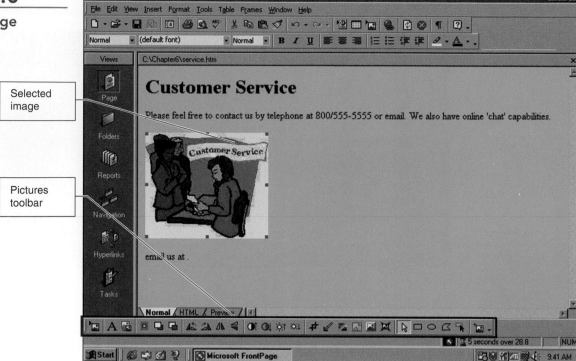

How Is a Hyperlink Inserted?

One of the most interesting features of any web page is the links found within it. A link, also called a **hyperlink,** lets you jump to other pages within the site or other pages elsewhere on the Web with a mouse click. A link can be one or more words, a whole image, or any part of an image. A link attached to a specific area in an image is called a **hotspot.** In most cases, you will be able to identify a link by its appearance (or the appearance of the mouse pointer) in the following ways:

- Blue, underlined text **B** if you have not clicked the link; a light purple if you have clicked the link.

- Pointer changes from ⌖ to 👆 when placed over text or image containing a link.

You can create a hyperlink using the same software used to build your website.

Steps

1. Click to the left of **.** in the **e-mail us at** line. The hyperlink will be inserted at the insertion point.

2. Click the **Hyperlink** button 🔘 on the Standard toolbar. The Create Hyperlink dialog box opens, as shown in Figure 6.9. To create a link to a web page, you could type in the address in the URL text box. You can also create a link that lets a visitor send you e-mail.

3. Click the **Make a hyperlink that sends E-mail** button, 💾 type **cs@jewelry-for-you.com** in the **Type an E-mail address** text box, as

Click to create a
link to a new page

Click to create an
e-mail link

Click to create a
link to a file on
your computer

Click to create a
link to a web URL

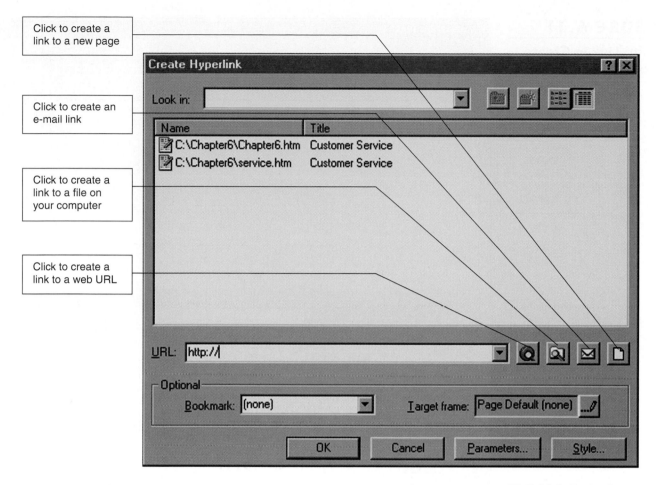

FIGURE 6.9

Create Hyperlink
Dialog Box

FIGURE 6.10

Create E-Mail
Hyperlink Dialog Box

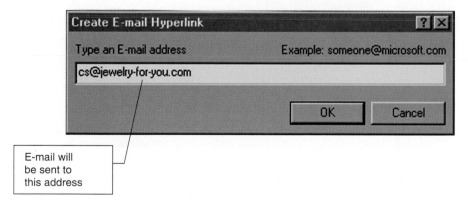

E-mail will
be sent to
this address

shown in Figure 6.10, then click **OK.** The Create Hyperlink dialog box is
completed, as seen in Figure 6.11.

4. Click **OK.** The Create Hyperlink dialog box closes and the hyperlink is
displayed in the page, as shown in Figure 6.12.

5. Click the **Save** button 🖫 on the Standard toolbar.

FIGURE 6.11

Mailto Link in Create
Hyperlink Dialog Box

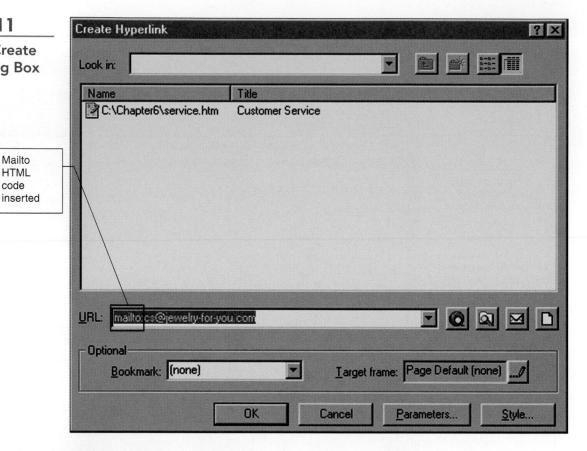

FIGURE 6.12

Hyperlink in Web Page

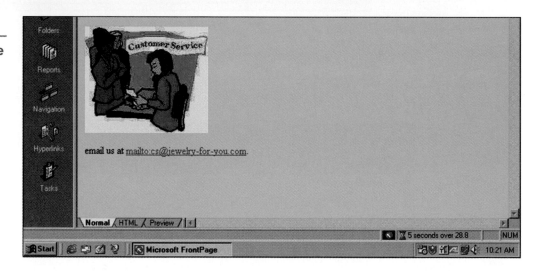

How Are Multimedia Files Used?

Multimedia links that let you enjoy full-motion video, sound, and radio files have become more prevalent, and more sophisticated, as the Internet has matured. There are many sites catering to a diverse audience. You can find up-to-the-minute news broadcasts, both visual and auditory, movie trailers, and live video sessions.

Multimedia is dependent on **bandwidth,** the amount of data that can be received by a remote computer at a given moment. Data bandwidth capability is analogous to the diameter of a pipe. A pipe that is too small causes water to back up. Too little bandwidth means it can take a long time to download a file; in addition, a video may appear jerky and sound may break up. Running multimedia can drain the resources of a computer, as performance is dependent on chip speed, available memory, and the recipient's Internet connection.

> **E-tip**
> Of course, you have no control over the bandwidth available to your site visitors, but you should be aware of the limitations of the medium.

What Kind of Sites Are Available?

There are sites featuring multimedia that cater to many media types and many tastes. Figure 6.13 shows a site that features radio, movie trailers, and music, as well as the tools you need to make these files work.

> **E-tip**
> Offering the necessary multimedia tools—or links to sites that have them—is a great value to add to a multimedia page.

The radio page of this website, shown in Figure 6.14, lets you listen to live broadcasts that you normally couldn't hear due to distance limitations.

The immediacy of the Web makes it an ideal venue for news of any kind. While many portals feature hyperlinks to stories about current events, many also feature full-motion video or links to sites that carry multimedia files. Figure 6.15 displays a news website that offers an interactive element as well as full-motion video and sound clips.

FIGURE 6.13

Multimedia Website

Available multimedia

FIGURE 6.14

Radio Website

FIGURE 6.15

Interactive News Page

Click for interactive elements

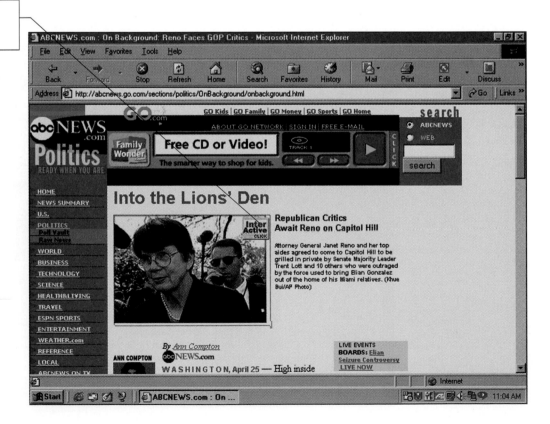

What Is a Form?

A form is used to collect data, whether it is in person or over the Internet. On a web page, individual **fields** are used to record responses to questions. When the form is completed, it is submitted to a website that tallies the information. Table 6.3 shows commonly used form elements that can be added using commands on FrontPage's Insert menu.

Where Can I Find Forms?

In an eBusiness, data can be gathered when subscribers join a site or orders are placed. Form elements can be found everywhere. One of the uses of a form can be seen in Figure 6.16, in which you can subscribe to receive a daily e-mail from Peter Jennings at ABC News. This form collects basic data and makes it easy to unsubscribe from the list. Figure 6.17 shows a form used to search for available domain names.

How Should a Form Be Designed?

There are several important considerations you should be aware of when designing a form.

* Know the purpose of gathering the data. Know what data you want, and waste no time with extraneous questions.
* Show consideration to the form respondent. The person filling out the form is doing you a favor; don't take advantage of it. Ask a few short questions, and

Name	Button
One-line text box	
Scrolling text box	
Check box	
Radio button	
Drop-down menu	
Push button	

TABLE 6.3

Common Form Elements

FIGURE 6.16

ABC News Subscription Form

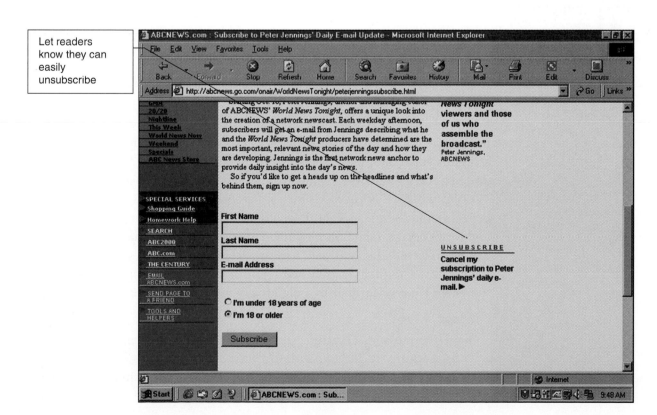

Let readers know they can easily unsubscribe

FIGURE 6.17

Domain Name Search
Form

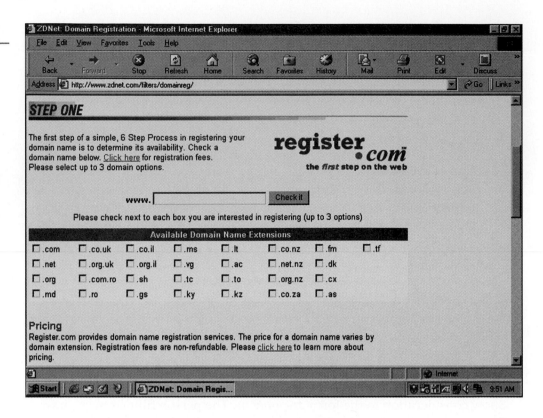

let the respondent know up front how many questions will be asked and how
long it should take.

- Questions should be in the form of selections rather than fill-in text fields.
  This will make the analysis of the data easier since the
  answers will be consistent. By using text fields, a
  respondent could list his or her home state as MA, ma,
  Mass., mass, massachusetts, or Massachusetts.

 Offering choices assures you of more
consistent data and makes it easier for
the respondent to complete the form.

How Is a Form Created?

FrontPage makes it easy to create a form. Using form elements in the Insert
menu, you can add individual fields where you want them. The first step in creating the form is to place the form element on the page. The form appears as a
dotted border, and you can add as many elements as you want within that border.

Collected data is usually sent to a website where it is tallied. To make this
process more efficient, FrontPage creates the form outline, including a Submit
and Reset button. The Submit button is used to send the data to a server where it
can be collected and analyzed, and the Reset button allows the respondent to set
the responses to their original settings. You can create a form in FrontPage using
the Form Page Wizard, or by individually inserting fields in a page.

Steps

1. Verify that **service.htm** is the active web page. You can use this page as an
   opportunity to gather data from your customers. Basic data, such as
   gender and geographic location, can be useful when marketing your
   eBusiness.

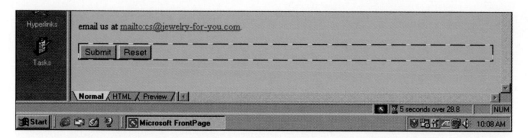

FIGURE 6.18

Initial Form Element

2. Click the line **e-mail us at,** click **Insert** on the menu bar, point to **Form,** then click **Form.** A Submit and Reset button display surrounded by dotted line, as shown in Figure 6.18. Since the Submit and Reset buttons are generally the last items in a form, the cursor is automatically placed to the left of the Submit button. The dotted line represents the border of the form and will not display in the Preview screen or on the web. Additional fields can be entered within the dotted border.

3. Type **Would you please provide us with some information?,** press **Enter, Are you male or female?,** press **Enter, In what area of the US do you live?,** press **Enter.** You can simplify the form process for your reader by inserting radio buttons and text boxes.

4. Click to the **left of male,** click **Insert** on the menu bar, point to **Form,** then click **Radio Button.** A selected radio button appears to the left of male.

5. Press and hold **Ctrl,** press [→] twice, click **Insert** on the menu bar, point to **Form,** then click **Radio Button.** An unselected radio button appears to the left of female. You can add a text box for the remaining question.

6. Click [↓], press **End,** click **Insert** on the menu bar, point to **Form,** then click **One-Line Text Box.** The text box is added to the form. Compare your screen to Figure 6.19.

7. Click the **Save** button 🖫 on the Standard toolbar, then click the **Preview** tab. Your screen should look like Figure 6.20.

How Can I Modify a Form?

Modifying a FrontPage form is similar to making modifications in any web page or word processing document. Text can be deleted or added, and objects can be deleted or inserted. Like graphic images, form fields are objects. When selected, a form field is surrounded by handles.

To offer form respondents choices, you can replace a text field with a drop-down menu. When you add a drop-down menu, you have to specify the choices that will be offered, and which choice is the default, or automatic, selection.

Steps

1. Click the **Normal** tab, then click the **one-line** text box on the form. Handles surround the text box. The handles indicate that the object is selected. You can delete an object by pressing the **Delete** key.

2. Press **Delete.** You can add a drop-down menu to give readers limited, consistent choices.

Because this field was just added, you could also delete it using the Undo 🔙 key.

FIGURE 6.19

Fields Placed in Form

Radio button

Default selection

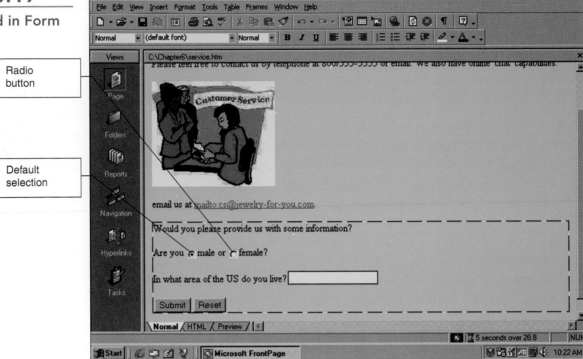

FIGURE 6.20

Form in Preview Screen

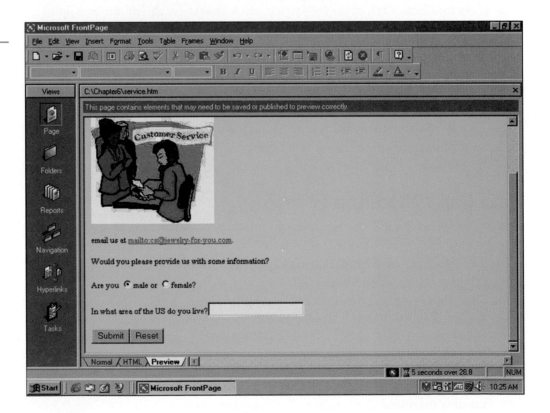

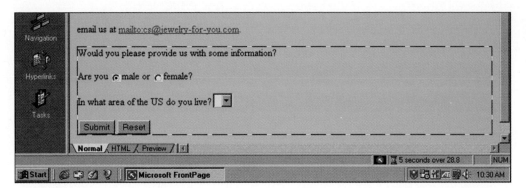

FIGURE 6.21

Text Box Replaced
with Drop-Down Menu

FIGURE 6.22

Drop-Down Menu
Properties Dialog Box

Indicates
default
selection

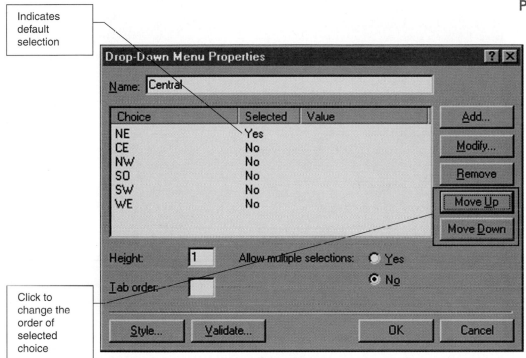

Click to
change the
order of
selected
choice

3. Click **Insert** on the menu bar, point to **Form,** then click **Drop-Down Menu.** An empty drop-down field displays, as shown in Figure 6.21.

4. Right-click the **drop-down** field, then click **Form Field Properties.** The Drop-Down Menu Properties dialog box displays.

5. Type **Northeast,** click **Add,** type **NE** in the **Choice** text box, click the **Selected radio** button, then click **OK.**

6. Repeat step 5 using Figure 6.22 as a guide, then click **OK.** All the drop-down list choices have been added. Compare your screen to Figure 6.23.

7. Click the **Save** button 💾 on the Standard toolbar; click the **Preview in browser** button 🔍 in the Standard toolbar; scroll down to view the form if necessary; then click the drop-down arrow. Your form should look like the Figure 6.24.

FIGURE 6.23

Completed Form

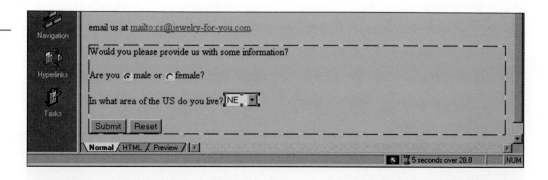

FIGURE 6.24

Form in Browser

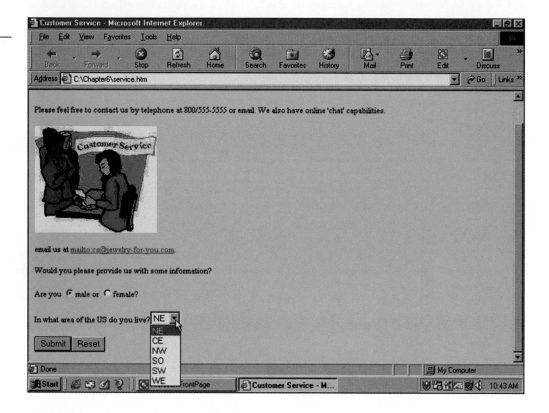

Checkpoint

The availability of digital cameras, scanners, and powerful web editors such as Front-Page make it possible for more people to design and create their own exciting websites. Before these innovations were available, it was obvious who the professional web page designers were. Only those who knew the magic incantations could create dynamic pages. And as if scanners and cameras aren't enough, you can find a wide variety of professional-looking images on the Web.

Web pages can be created and modified easily using Microsoft FrontPage, as well as other programs. Hyperlinks, graphic images, and form elements can all be inserted and modified using toolbar buttons and menu commands.

Keys

graphic image   lossy   hotspot
scanner   intellectual property multimedia
digital camera   picture file   bandwidth
clipart   hyperlink   field

Milestones

Complete the following statements:

1. A graphic _____ is a picture in electronic format.
2. An image format that discards data as it compresses the file is referred to as _____.
3. The file extension for the Tagged Image File Format is _____.
4. Corporate knowledge or a procedure are examples of _____ property.
5. An image is sometimes called a _____ file.
6. You can jump to other pages using a link, also called a _____.
7. A link specific to an area in an image is called a _____.
8. Full-motion video and sound files are examples of _____ files.
9. Collect information by placing _____ in a form.
10. When a field is selected, it is surrounded by _____.

Complete the following exercises:

1. Find and print three examples of websites that feature forms. Critique these forms, pointing out positive and negative features of each.
2. What are the ethical ramifications of collecting data on a website? Does a website owner owe readers full disclosure as to how the data will be used? Are questionnaires an invasion of privacy? Use your favorite word processor to answer these questions in a document called Ethics.

Your Turn

Use FrontPage to design a form for a fictional real estate eBusiness called yournewhome.com. Although you can add additional fields, make sure you include fields for gender, age group, price range, number of bedrooms, number of bathrooms, and number of children. Save the form as ynhform.htm.

CHAPTER 7

Perfecting

How Can I Improve a Web Page?

The organization and delivery of information on web pages is vital to getting the message to your readers. You want the pages in your website to be attractive and well designed, yet informative.

There are several organizational tools you can use to make the best use of space in your pages. You can use tables to organize information such as prices or options, and you can use frames to display multiple web pages in a single page. Microsoft FrontPage has a variety of frame templates that make construction of these pages simple.

The Jewelry-For-You site can utilize tables for its pricing information and can show two pages in a side-by-side format that will be easy to read without looking too busy.

Creating Advanced Web Pages

CHAPTER OUTLINE

Why Should I Use a Table?

How Is a Table Created?

How Can I Format a Table?

How Can I Use Colors and Borders?

How Can I Control Table Elements?

What Are Frames?

How Can I Build Framed Pages?

How Can I Include Links in My Site?

FIGURE 7.1

Working on Enhancements

Why Should I Use a Table?

A **table** is a grid consisting of columns and rows and can be used to organize tabular data such as pricing information or to control the display of text. Each individual box within the table is called a **cell.**

By hiding the grid, you can use a table to list information in a column and no one will ever know a table is present. Like regular text, table data can be formatted using attributes such as boldface, italics, or underlining.

Figure 7.2 shows a table used to display mortgage rate information. Some of the cells contain text that has been formatted in various colors, and some headings **span,** or extend, over several columns. The web page in Figure 7.3 contains a table with formatting as well as hyperlinks within the table cells.

Prior to the development of web editors such as Microsoft FrontPage, it was necessary to understand the HTML tags used to create a table. These codes (the <TABLE> code shows the initial and trailing tags) are listed in Table 7.1.

How Is a Table Created?

FrontPage makes it easy to create a table. There are two methods you can use: a button on the Standard toolbar or a command on the Table menu. Using the Table menu takes slightly more time but offers more options and flexibility. Regardless of which option you choose, you will be asked to specify the number of columns and rows you want. You can always change your mind and either add or delete columns or rows if you have miscalculated the table's dimensions.

FIGURE 7.2

Table Used in Web Page

Cell spans 2 columns

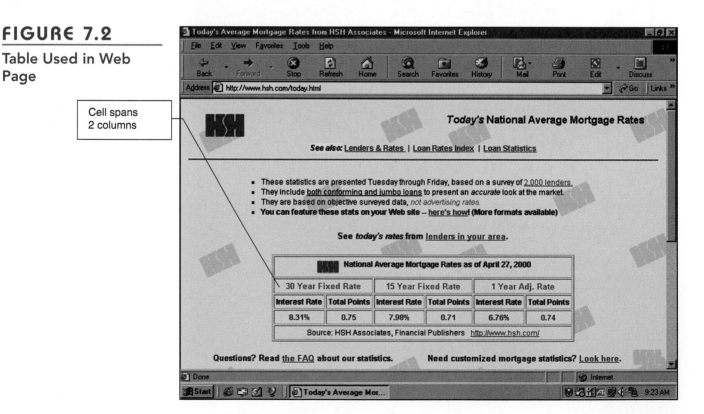

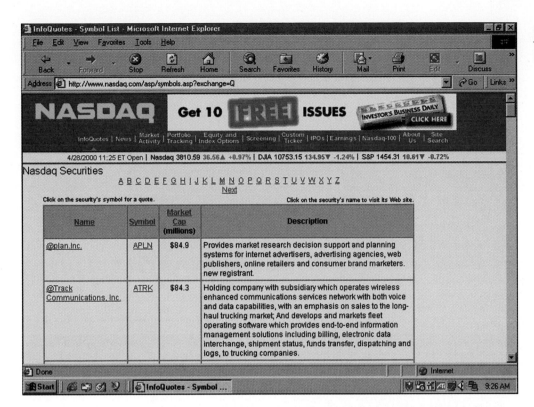

FIGURE 7.3

Hyperlinks in Table

TABLE 7.1

HTML Table Tags

Name	Function
<TABLE> </TABLE>	Surrounds all table codes
<TH>	Signifies the table header
<TR>	Defines each row
<TD>	Signifies each cell
COLSPAN	Determines column span
ALIGN	Determines text alignment

Steps

1. Start FrontPage, click the **Open** button 📂 on the Standard toolbar, locate the Project Files, click **Chapter7,** then click **Open.** The file opens, and you can save the file using a different name so you can repeat this exercise, if necessary.

2. Click **File** on the menu bar, click **Save As,** type **prices** in the File name text box, then click **Save.** The file has been renamed. You can create a table using the Table menu. You can also create a table using the Insert Table button 🔲 on the Standard toolbar. This method is quicker but offers fewer options.

3. Press [↓] twice, click **Table** on the menu bar, point to **Insert,** then click **Table.** The Insert Table dialog box opens, as shown in Figure 7.4.

FIGURE 7.4

Insert Table Dialog Box

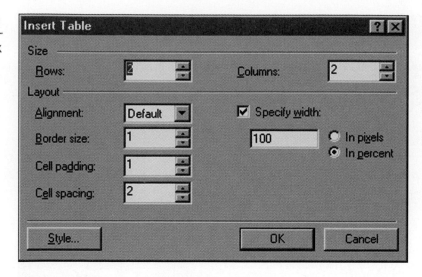

FIGURE 7.5

Table Data

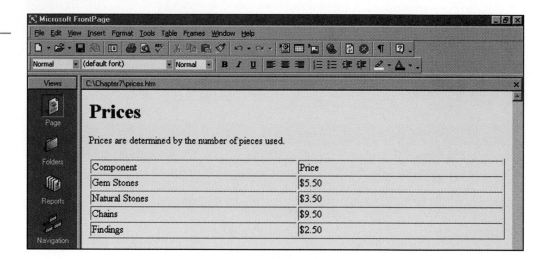

4. Type **5** in the Rows text box, then click **OK.** A two-column, five-row table appears on the page. The cursor is positioned in the top left table cell.

5. Type **Component** in the top left cell, press **Tab,** type **Price,** then press **Tab.** Complete the table using the data in Figure 7.5.

You can add a new row to a table by positioning the pointer in the last cell of the last row, then pressing Tab.

6. Click the **Save** button 🔳 on the Standard toolbar.

How Can I Format a Table?

There are many formatting options you can use in a table. You can change the attributes of the text within the table, such as changing the font and font color. You can also add attributes such as boldface, italics, and underlining. You can also change the width and color of the table and cell borders.

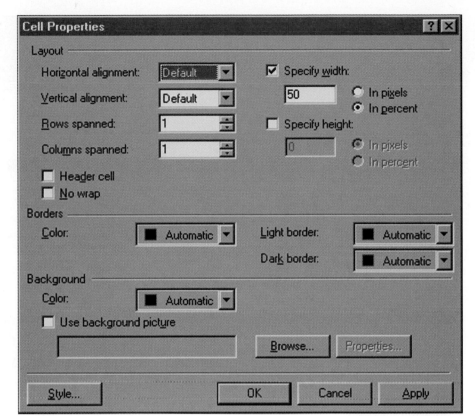

FIGURE 7.6

Cell Properties Dialog Box

Steps

1. Position the pointer to the left of Component, then click when pointer changes to ➡. The first row in the table is selected. You can apply formatting, such as boldface or italics, using button on the Formatting toolbar. You can also select a column or row by clicking Table on the menu bar, pointing to Select, then clicking Table, Column, Row, or Cell.

2. Click the **Bold** button **B** on the Formatting toolbar. The text in the selected cells becomes bold. To make the first row appear more dramatic, you can change the background color and text of the selected cells.

3. Click **Table** on the menu bar, point to **Properties,** then click **Cell.** The Cell Properties dialog box opens, as shown in Figure 7.6.

4. Click the **Background Color** list arrow, click the **Black** color box (the first box on the left in the row beneath Standard colors), then click **OK.** The selected row appears to be empty. You can now change the text color.

5. Click the **Font Color** list arrow **A** ▾ on the Formatting toolbar, click the **Yellow** color box (the first box on the left in the row above Document's Colors), then click any location in the table.

   Compare your screen to Figure 7.7. The column widths are much wider than is necessary, and making the columns narrower will improve the appearance of the table. You can automatically fit the column widths to the cell contents using the AutoFit feature.

6. Click **Table** on the menu bar, then click **AutoFit.** The columns in the table have been resized, as shown in Figure 7.8.

7. Click the **Save** button 💾 on the Standard toolbar.

FIGURE 7.7

Formatted Table Data

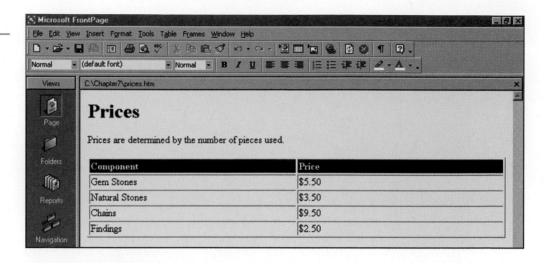

FIGURE 7.8

Resized Columns

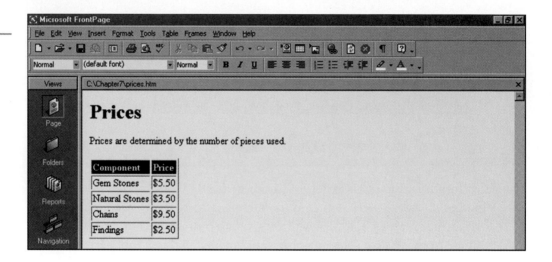

How Can I Use Colors and Borders?

Adding color to borders or cell backgrounds can make your table eye-catching. Some elements, such as border color and width, are controlled using the Table Properties dialog box. Using the Table menu, you can apply multiple changes without having to close and open the dialog box each time.

Steps

1. Verify that the cursor is still within the table. You can control the appearance of elements within the table using a command on the Table menu.

2. Click **Table** on the menu bar, point to **Properties,** then click **Table.** The Table Properties dialog box opens.

FIGURE 7.9

Color Applied to Table

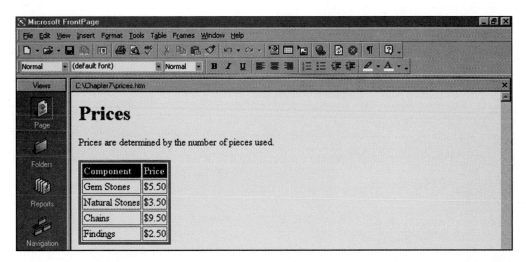

FIGURE 7.10

Table with Altered
Border Size

3. Click the **Borders Color** list arrow, click the **Blue** color box (the second box from the right in the row above Document's colors), then click **Apply.** The blue color is applied to the table while the dialog box remains open, as shown in Figure 7.9.

4. Double-click the **Size** text box, type **4,** then click **OK.** Compare your table to Figure 7.10.

5. Click the **Save** button on the Standard toolbar.

Click Apply to see the effects of a change without closing a dialog box.

How Can I Control Table Elements?

You can control the amount of space surrounding cell text, or **padding,** using the Table Properties dialog box. The table's background color is also controlled using this dialog box. The page background, however, is controlled using the Properties command on the Format menu.

Steps

1. Verify that the cursor is still within the table. You can change the padding, or amount of space that surrounds each cell.

2. Click **Table** on the menu bar, point to **Properties,** then click **Table.** The Table Properties dialog box opens.

3. Double-click the **Cell padding** text box, type **5,** then click **Apply.** Each table cell has additional space added, as shown in Figure 7.11. You can change the background of the table using the Table Properties dialog box.

 You can change the background of the page by clicking Format on the menu bar, then clicking Properties.

4. Click the **Background color** list arrow, click the **Yellow** color box (the first box on the left in the row above Document's colors), then click **OK.** Compare the colors and settings in your table to Figure 7.12.

5. Click the **Save** button 🖫 on the Standard toolbar.

FIGURE 7.11

Cell Padding Modified

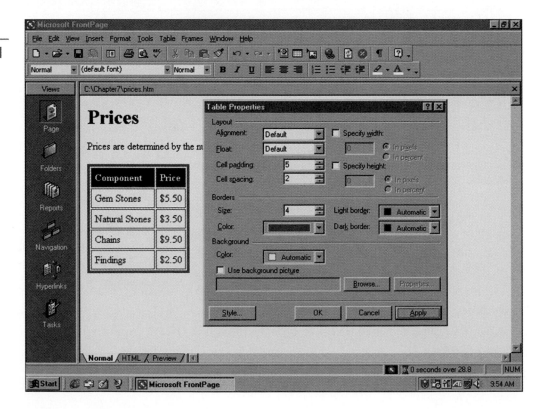

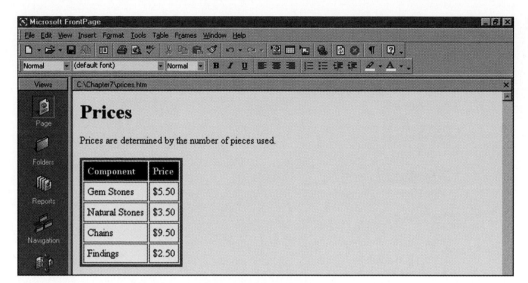

FIGURE 7.12

Table Background Color Changed

What Are Frames?

A **frame** is an independent window within a web page. While a standard web page has a single frame, you can display any number of frames, although you rarely see more than three frames. Depending on the type and amount of information within your pages, frames can allow you to present more data in a given space.

How Can I Use Frames?

Multiple frames can be set up horizontally or vertically, as shown in Figure 7.13. Notice that each frame has its own vertical scroll bars, while only the right-hand frame has a horizontal scroll bar. Scroll bars only appear if they are necessary, and if they have been programmed to appear.

The screen in Figure 7.14 contains three frames: two verticals and one horizontal. This page also contains a multimedia element that plays a recorded song. Each frame can be scrolled independently from the others. Figure 7.15 shows two horizontal frames, in which the top frame is stationary and almost invisible.

Are There Frame Design Considerations?

When creating any web page, you should always be thinking of the design and how it impacts your site. Some people feel that frames are gimmicky, and should not be used at all. Others feel that in small doses they can be quite effective.

When contemplating using frames, consider the following:

- Consider how much information you want to present and whether it will be well served by frames. If you pack too much information into a screen, you may overwhelm your readers.

- Using frames in your website should add value to your pages. A good case for using frames would be when it is helpful for users to see related information in a side-by-side environment.

- Be aware that some readers with visual or mental impairments may find frames confusing. In this event, you may want to offer a nonframed page alternative.

FIGURE 7.13

Two Frames in Web Page

Individual scroll bar for frame

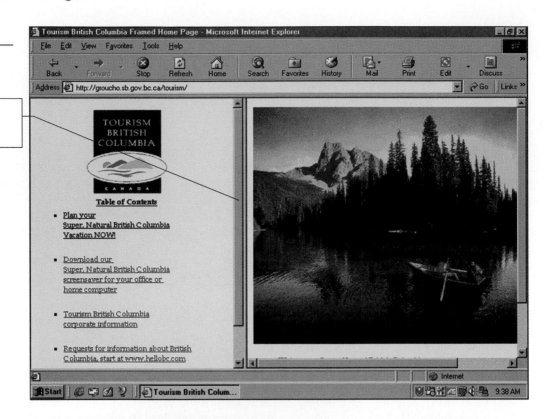

FIGURE 7.14

Three Frames with Multimedia Clip

Multimedia element

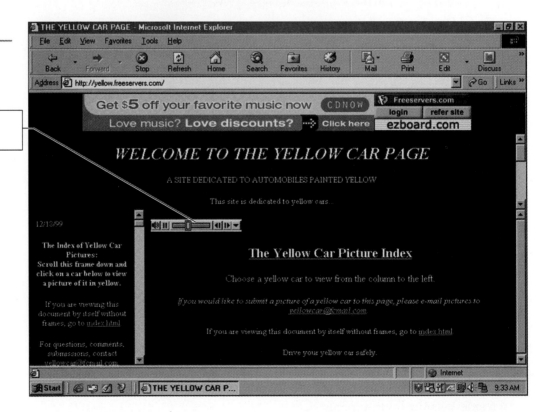

Stationery
frame

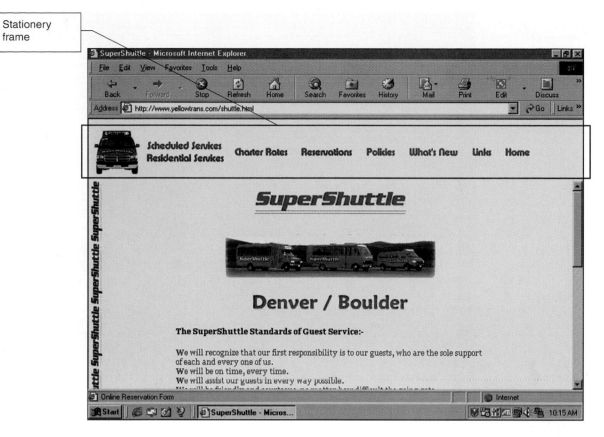

FIGURE 7.15

Borderless Frame in
Page

How Can I Build Framed Pages?

You can create framed pages easily with FrontPage. Since there are so many possible configurations for framed pages, you can choose the layout you want and assign web pages to their locations. Pages are assigned by clicking a button in a frame and then locating the file you want to use. If a page does not yet exist, you can create it on the fly.

Steps

1. Click **File** on the menu bar, point to **New,** then click **Page.** The New dialog box opens. A special tab exists to help you create framed pages.
2. Click the **Frames Pages** tab, click **Vertical Split,** as shown in Figure 7.16, then click **OK.** A new page, shown in Figure 7.17, displays. You can use the buttons in the frames to define the pages that will be displayed.
3. Click the **Set Initial Page** button in the left frame, click the **Look in** list arrow to locate the **creation.htm file,** then click **OK.** The creation file displays in the left frame.
4. Click the **Set Initial Page** button in the right frame, click the **Look in** list arrow to locate the **prices.htm file,** then click **OK.** Both files appear on the screen. Both frame widths do not have to be the same size, and you can change the width using your mouse.

Preview of selected layout

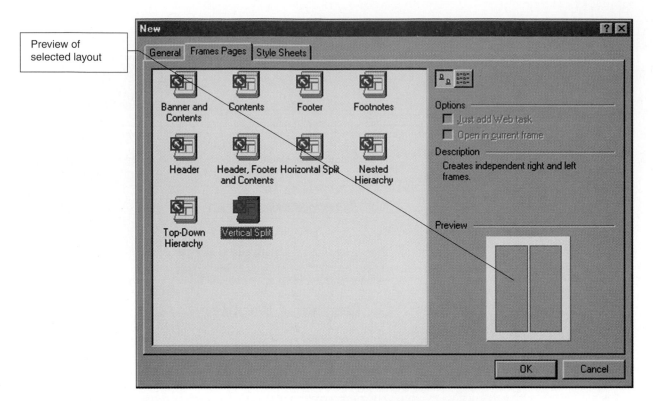

FIGURE 7.16

New Dialog Box

Active page is surrounded by a blue border

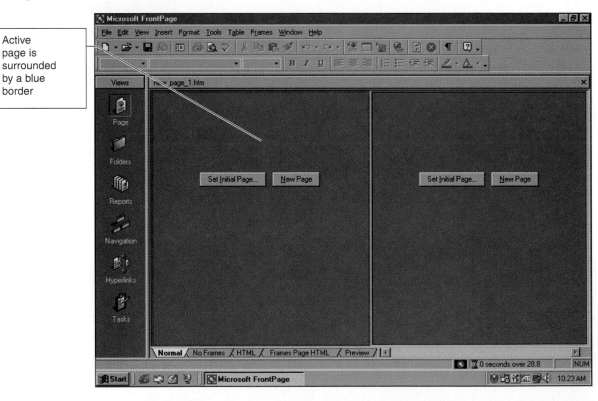

FIGURE 7.17

Page with Two Vertical Frames

5. Position the mouse to the left of the table so the pointer changes to ⟷ , then drag the pointer so it lies under the dimmed **Stop** button ⊗. Compare your frames to those in Figure 7.18. You can save the frame using the same method you use to save a web page.

6. Click the **Save** button 💾 on the Standard toolbar, then click the **Save in** list arrow to locate your files, type **frame** in the File name list box, then click **Save.**

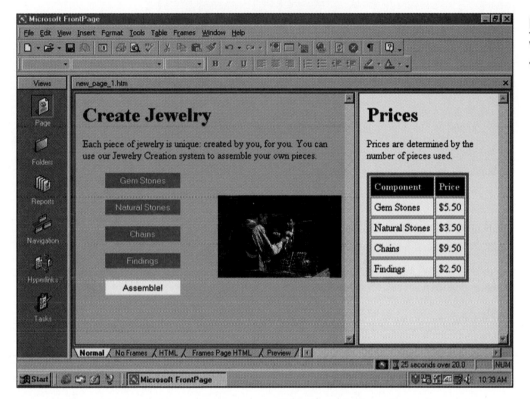

FIGURE 7.18

Web Pages Assigned to Frames

CONTROLLING A FRAME

You can prevent readers of your site from resizing framed pages using the Frame Properties dialog box (see Figure 7.19). To open this dialog box, right-click the frame you want to control, then click Frame Properties. When the dialog box opens, click the Resizable in browser check box to prevent the frame from being resized. You can also control whether or not scroll bars are displayed by clicking the Show scroll bars list arrow and selecting the option you want.

FIGURE 7.19

Frame Properties
Dialog Box

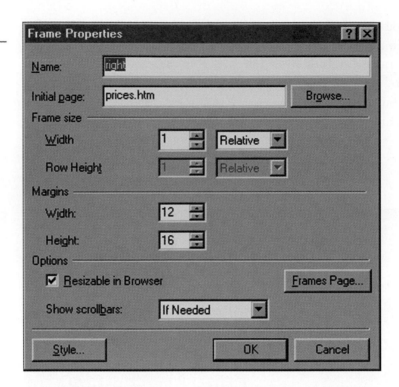

How Can I Include Links in My Site?

Links can be created that let you jump to other sites or send an e-mail. When you insert text in a page, think about how the text will be used and whether or not it should contain a link.

Steps

1. Click the **prices** frame, then click **below the table.** Before creating the hyperlink, you will insert descriptive text.

2. Type **Click to learn what is available.** This text will be turned into a hyperlink and will display in blue underlined text. Once the hyperlink is clicked, the blue will display as purple, or some other color.

3. Select the newly typed text, then click the **Hyperlink** button on the Standard toolbar. The Hyperlink dialog box opens, as shown in Figure 7.20.

4. Type **jewelrysupplier.com** (after the http://) in the URL text box, click **OK,** then click any location in the table. The text displays as a hyperlink, as shown in Figure 7.21.

5. Click the **Save** button on the Standard toolbar.

6. Click **File** on the menu bar, then click **Exit.**

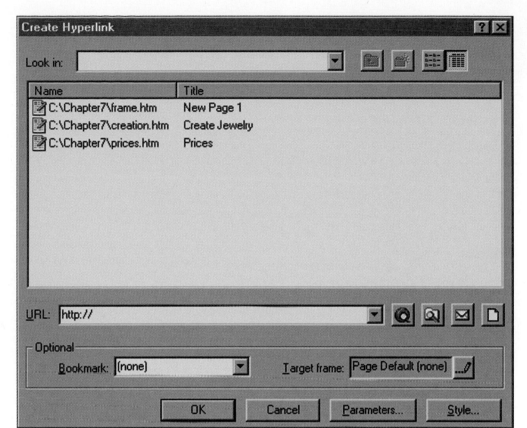

FIGURE 7.20

Create Hyperlink
Dialog Box

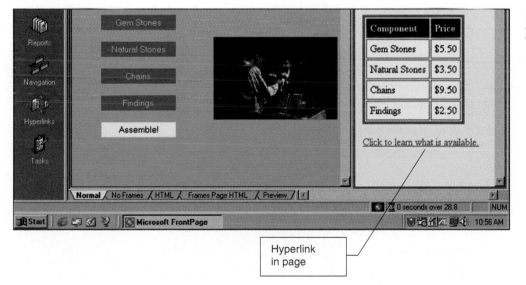

FIGURE 7.21

Text Displays as
Hyperlink

Checkpoint

Any web page can inform, but you can add real spark to your pages using techniques such as tables, frames, and hyperlinks. Tables are useful when organizing text and data and can give your pages a professional, tidy feel.

You can use frames to pack more information into a screen, as well as provide helpful data in a side-by-side atmosphere. Often it is helpful to see several screens at once to digest information and make selections.

Keys

table	span	frame
cell	padding	

Milestones

Complete the following statements:

1. A _____ is a grid consisting of columns and rows.

2. A table can be formatted using _____ such as boldface and underlining.

3. Each individual box in a table is called a(n) _____.

4. In FrontPage, you can create a table using a toolbar button or a command on the _____ menu.

5. Resize table columns using a command on the _____ menu.

6. The amount of space surrounding cell text is called _____.

7. An independent window within a web page is called a(n) _____.

8. You can prevent a reader from resizing a frame using the Frame _____ dialog box.

9. Click the Show _____ list arrow to control the appearance of scroll bars.

10. Hyperlinked text appears in the color _____ and is underlined.

Complete the following exercises:

1. Find and print three examples of websites that feature frames. Critique these pages, pointing out positive and negative features of each.

2. Including hyperlinks in your web pages adds value for your readers. What, if any, are the drawbacks of including these links?

Your Turn

Use FrontPage to design a web page (containing at least two frames) for greatpetsupplies.com, a fictional pet supply eBusiness. Include any information you feel is necessary. Save any pages you create as GPS-1, GPS-2, and so forth in the designated location.

CHAPTER 8

Operating

What Does It Take to Run an eBusiness?

You've written the business plan and the marketing plan. You've designed and created your website. Maybe you've even included several bells and whistles that make your pages look cool. So now you're done, right? Nothing left to do but count the money as it flows in? Perhaps there is still more to be learned.

Running a business requires some accounting and management knowledge. Whether you are running an eBusiness or a more conventional bricks-and-mortar business, you still want to make a profit, and you still need to manage your employees and subcontractors. If you are working remotely, you also need special skills that allow you to telecommute effectively.

More than ever before, you may find that there are just not enough hours in the day for all the things you need to do.

Running an eBusiness

CHAPTER OUTLINE

How Much Accounting Should I Know?

What Management Techniques Are Helpful?

How Can I Work from a Distance?

How Can I Get Help?

THINGS TO DO TODAY

15 Exercise class at 7:30

FIGURE 8.1

Not Enough Hours in the Day

How Much Accounting Should I Know?

More than likely, you are aware that a certified public accountant (CPA) studies exhausting amounts of material for many years and then must pass a very difficult standardized test before he or she is permitted to open a practice.

You're probably wondering just how much accounting you actually need to know. After all, if you're like most businesspeople, you are probably planning on retaining a CPA to fulfill your tax requirements and complete your annual report. So why should you even try to understand this difficult subject? Like any other segment of your business, you should have at least a basic understanding of how your profits and losses are calculated. If your company produces a product, you will probably hire people to complete each task, but you will still want to know a little about each step of the process.

Although two of the primary functions of accounting relate to taxes and payroll, there are other important uses of this knowledge base. In a sense, accounting data provide the ultimate in information systems, as you will use this information to make a multitude of decisions that affect every aspect of your business.

So, what is the answer to the initial question? You should know enough accounting to understand how to run your business and make intelligent decisions. You can supplement your existing knowledge by reading a variety of websites, such as the one shown in Figure 8.2.

Are There Different Kinds of Accounting?

While there are many subsets within the accounting discipline, the two basic distinctions are external and internal accounting. People outside your organization, generally use external or **financial accounting.** Auditors or CPAs compile data

FIGURE 8.2

Nolo's Accounting Basics

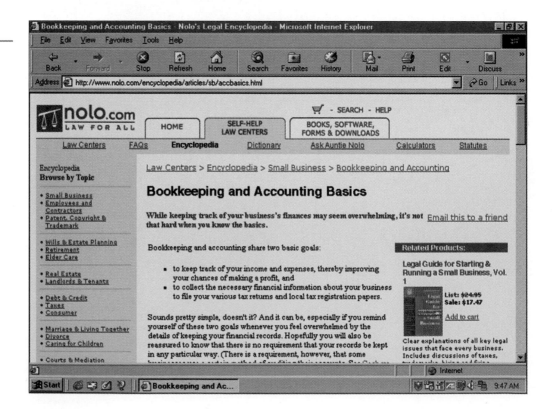

using Generally Accepted Accounting Principles (GAAP), which ensure that the accounting is accurate, objective, and comparable. A typical example of financial accounting is a report that details profits and losses during a particular time period, which might be given to bankers, board members, or potential investors. The goals of financial reporting are as follows:

- To provide information that gives decision makers a reasonable level of business knowledge.
- To help assess future cash flows.
- To identify and value economic resources.

People within your organization will want to see periodic reports that help them make decisions about material purchases, new hires, and other budgetary issues. This is considered internal or **management accounting.**

What Are Basic Accounting Concepts?

Whether your business produces a product or sells a service, there are certain basic terms with which you should be familiar. The primary characteristics for judging whether accounting information is useful are relevance and reliability, and the secondary characteristics are comparability and consistency.

In accounting, most of the data are boiled down to this simple equation: Assets = Liabilities + Owner's equity. An **asset** is something of value that is owned by the firm and will provide probable future economic benefit; a **liability** is something owed by the firm, requiring future sacrifice of economic benefits. **Equity** is the residual interest in the assets that remains after deducting the entity's liabilities. **Owner's equity** is what is left over: the difference between assets and liabilities.

Revenues are the inflow of assets that result from the sale of goods or services.

Expenses are the consumption of assets needed to generate revenues. The **net income (or loss)** is the difference between revenues and expenses.

These terms, and others, are shown in Figure 8.3. Table 8.1 also lists some common accounting terms.

What Happens in Accounting?

Accounting has processes and rules that must be obeyed. There are identifiable steps in the accounting cycle for any given time period:

1. Transactions are identified and measured.
2. Transactions are listed chronologically, called **journalizing.**
3. Transactions are accumulated, called **posting.**
4. Accounts are divided into categories, called a **chart of accounts,** and are aggregated and listed to create an unadjusted trial balance.
5. Adjustments are made to achieve a proper matching of revenues and expenses.
6. Accounts are aggregated and listed to create an **adjusted trial balance.**
7. Statements are prepared.
8. Revenue and expense account balances are closed for the time period.

FIGURE 8.3

More Accounting
Basics

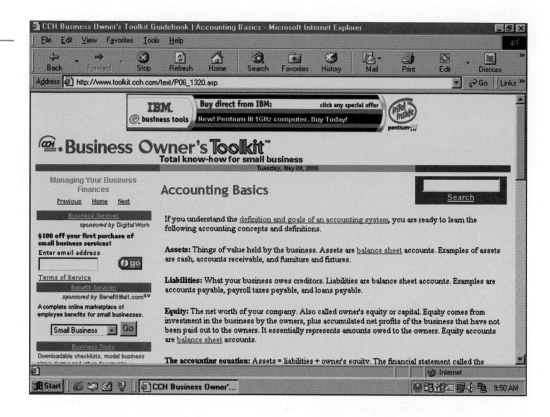

TABLE 8.1

Accounting Terms

Term	Definition
Going concern	Assuming that a company will remain in business
Periodicity	Using measurable, accepted time segments
Conservatism	Having contingency plans and being pessimistic in estimates
Realization	Entering, or *booking*, assets and liabilities into the system
Consistency	Using equilivant comparison assumptions
Materiality	Reporting essential information; ignoring trivial data
Economic entity	Assuming that business activities are separate and distinct from those activities of its owners

What Financial Statements Are Necessary?

To evaluate the financial health of a business, four statements are generally provided to outside sources:

- Balance sheet
- Income statement
- Statement of cash flows
- Statement of owner's equity

What Management Techniques Are Helpful?

Management and leadership skills are hot topics in today's entrepreneurial marketplace. With very little effort, you can find a host of seminars promoted to teach

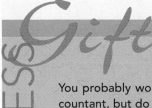

BUSINESS LAW

You probably wouldn't dream of starting a business without consulting an accountant, but do you need a lawyer? In addition to helping you choose and set up your corporate structure (sole proprietorship, partnership, or corporation), an attorney can provide you with business advice and prevent unforeseen liabilities. If your business requires patents or needs protection due to the use of intellectual property, your attorney should either be able to help you or provide a referral.

Your attorney should be able to help with all aspects of your business, including creating a structure that minimizes your personal liability in the event the business fails. A lawyer can also help you with product liability, warrantees, and advertising decisions and should minimize you and your business exposure to damages.

how to be an effective leader and good manager. Why, then, do so many people hate their bosses? With the number of seminars and self-help books available, shouldn't we have taught everyone how to be an effective leader by now?

Often the problem is not in the training but in the trainees. You not only have to want to be an effective leader, but you must see your flaws and, most important, be willing and able to make corrections.

What Makes a Leader Effective?

What qualities do you admire in a leader? The hands-down guru of management training is Stephen Covey, whose website is shown in Figure 8.4. Think of a leader, either well known or obscure, and make a list of what you feel makes this person great. In addition to being honest, supportive, and fair-minded, effective leaders have the ability to inspire, to enlist others in a shared vision, and to develop a collaborative effort.

The role of leadership within a company cannot be understated. As simple as the title implies, a *leader* shows others the way. Leadership can be as complex as outlining a sophisticated business plan, complete with time lines and financial forecasts, and as simple as keeping formality to a minimum and calling co-workers by their first names. The leader sets the tone and is the ultimate role model for the organization. If the leader isn't devoted to the company, the employees won't be.

Whether the destination is a hike in the woods or bringing a new product to market, the leader gets us there. The leader's abilities determine just how pleasurable and enriching that trip will be. A truly effective leader shares his or her vision with the group and makes that vision a reality. Sometimes the leader is forced to make unpopular decisions, such as firing team members.

An effective leader does not look for yes-men who only agree. Challenge and dissent make team members think, bringing new ideas and new methods to light. An effective leader is not afraid to challenge the status quo and is not leery of ideas that come from others. The changing landscape of the leadership market can be seen in Figure 8.5.

THE EDGE

Some of the best leadership tips are found not in how-to guides but in the biographies of effective leaders.

THE EDGE

Bureaucracy and routines are surefire ways of inhibiting creativity. They discourage risk taking, an essential element in the creative process.

FIGURE 8.4

Franklin Covey Website. Franklin Covey Is Not a Virtual Organization. However, This Is an Example of a Small Portion of Their Website.

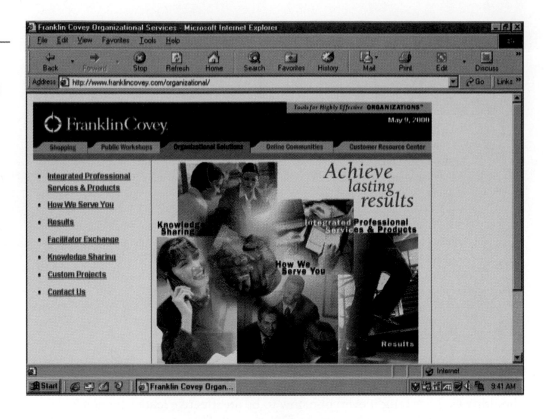

FIGURE 8.5

The Role of Leadership

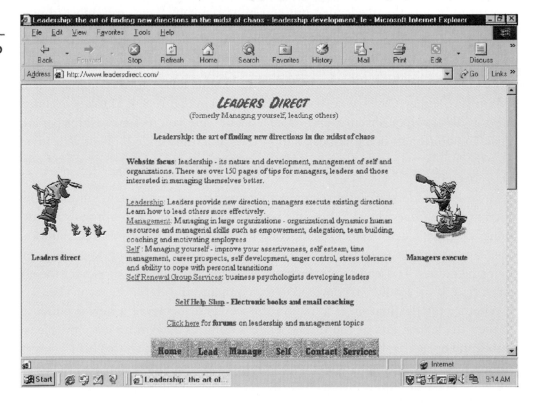

VIRTUAL ORGANIZATIONS

Communication within any organization is vital. In today's business venue, you may be asked to work within a **virtual organization.** This is a group in which team members are scattered throughout the state, country, or globe. Face-to-face meetings are not necessary; and total ownership in the project, by each team member, is essential.

Make sure the rules of communication are simple and understood. If you have questions, ask. If you don't understand something, ask. If you question the management of any portion of the project, including areas that are not your own, ask.

In order for a virtual organization to be successful, each team member must be self-motivated and willing to take initiative. In essence, each team member must be willing to assume the leadership role and must *own* the entire project. By each team member assuming ownership, each one is responsible for the overall quality of the project.

> **E-tip**
> Professionalism, discipline, and good communication skills are the keys to being a successful member of a virtual organization.

How Can I Work from a Distance?

Working from a remote location—at home or from an office not at your company's central location—or **telecommuting,** is a recent phenomenon. This new form of working can mean freedom to workers and employers alike. It can also mean disaster if it is not planned and managed correctly.

With increasing frequency, employers are encouraging employees to work several days a week from home. While most of us know how to function successfully in an office environment, this increasing trend toward working independently demands that we update our skills. Telecommuting from a **SOHO** (small office, home office) requires specific tools and skills. Many others are exploring the entrepreneurial world and are establishing their own businesses. Many publications that give insight to telecommuting are available on the Web, as shown in Figure 8.6.

How Can I Telecommute Effectively?

How do you become an effective telecommuter? Can anyone develop the necessary skills? Those who work remotely tend to be more mature workers who can make decisions and do not want or need handholding. There are many traits common to telecommuters. They tend to

- Work well independently and need little supervision.
- Have good time management skills.
- Like to make decisions and show initiative.
- Have the ability to work in relative isolation.
- Recognize trouble signs and ask for assistance.

Of course, these attributes do not guarantee success, but these are good building blocks.

FIGURE 8.6

Smart Valley
Telecommuting Guide

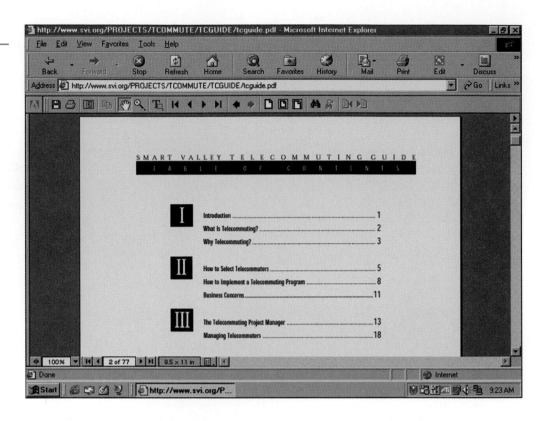

Why Is Telecommuting So Difficult?

You, and your fellow telecommuters, will develop your own office culture using the telephone and e-mail.

As a telecommuter, you may initially feel like a fish out of water since you are removed from the day-to-day office culture. You'll miss the daily interactions and the water cooler gossip. See Figure 8.7 for a website that deals with this issue. Since you are out of the mainstream, you'll have to depend on your decision-making abilities and learn to recognize when you're floundering.

Once you recognize that you need help, you must learn to ask for it, and quickly. In a standard office situation, a supervisor can use his or her managerial skills to spot the signs that a subordinate needs assistance. As a telecommuter, there is no one to sense when you are in trouble: you have to recognize this yourself and take the appropriate action.

How Should I Interact with Teammates?

Effective telecommuters exhibit many leadership skills. Many telecommuters work in teams and need to be in touch with their teammates. Unless you have been told otherwise, few employers will object to interaction among teammates.

Any time you have two or more people working together, the conditions are ripe to have one member emerge as a leader. You can seize the initiative and use the following tools to make your team more cohesive:

* Make sure you communicate periodically with each team member. This can be as innocuous as a weekly telephone call or e-mail through which you just touch base. You can also circulate weekly progress reports that keep

FIGURE 8.7

Finding Friends

teammates in the loop. Without this communication, each member will feel as though he or she is working in a vacuum.

- Follow up real or virtual meetings with e-mail. Send a copy to all meeting attendees and your teammates. It's important that all team members are on the same page.

- Let teammates know your schedule. No one expects you to be chained to your desk 24 hours/7 days a week. If you are going to be out of the office, circulate an e-mail that lets people know your availability. State whether you will be checking your voice- or e-mail, and include alternate telephone numbers if someone needs to reach you.

Telecommuting may mean doing some things differently. Table 8.2 lists some common tasks and how a telecommuter can handle them.

How Should I Interact with My Manager?

The rules of managing employees are altered in the telecommuting environment. A telecommuter must learn to speak up when something is wrong. It is also your responsibility to let your manager know about the adequacy of your workload.

Many managers depend on *face time* to judge how a team or project is functioning. Face time is partially, if not totally, eliminated. For insight into dealing with your manager, see the website shown in Figure 8.8.

Managers, like the telecommuters themselves, have to learn how to develop other skills. Rather than judging an employee by a facial expression, managers can learn to read vocal tones and general attitudes.

TABLE 8.2

Telecommuting
Equivalents

In the Office You . . .	As a Telecommuter, You . . .
Write a note	Send an e-mail
Leave a voice message	Leave a voice message; send an e-mail
Fax a page	Send a document as an attachment, or fax from your PC
Ship a document overnight	Send a document as an attachment, fax from PC, or upload a document to a website

FIGURE 8.8

Working with Your
Manager

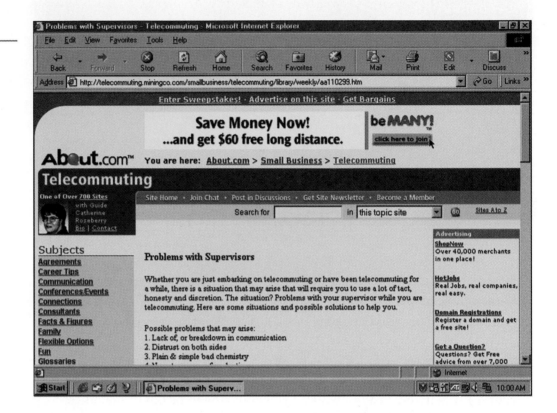

SMALL OFFICE, HOME OFFICE

There are oodles of articles on setting up a home office. Many of these articles go into great detail about the importance of a dedicated work area equipped with ergonomic furniture to ensure your comfort. In addition, you also need to make sure your work area is quiet and free from distractions. Use the Web to help set up your home office. The page shown in Figure 8.9 helps you set up a home network.

Many people who attempt telecommuting can't resist the temptation of attending to those dishes in the dishwasher or the clothes in the dryer. This is particularly difficult for those who work at home sporadically, since not being at the office seems special and unusual.

E-tip Don't think of your home office as being *at home*. Think of it as *going to your place of work*, as if it was an office in a building across town.

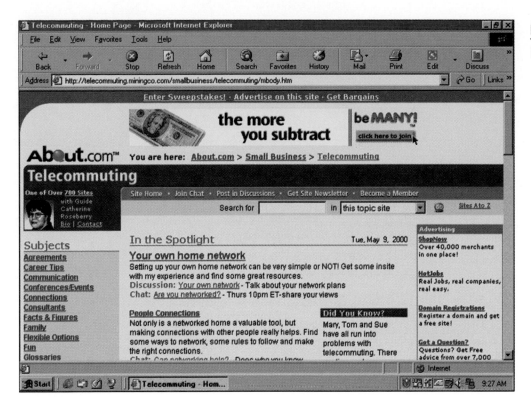

FIGURE 8.9

Home Network Hints

How Can I Get Help?

The Internet is the largest arsenal you have to get help for you and your eBusiness. Almost every government agency has a website that contains seemingly endless data. These websites are great sources of information, often having many links to other related sites.

The home page for the U.S. Small Business Administration is shown in Figure 8.10. This site features information on starting and financing a business, as well as links to helpful government resources.

Virtual user groups and local groups of businesspeople provide support that is there for the taking. The publication shown in Figure 8.11 encourages regional businesspeople to use its member base as a means of creating forums in which ideas are shared. Other such publications exist.

Private organizations, such as the one shown in Figure 8.12, offer additional resources on websites that can help you develop your business contacts.

FIGURE 8.10

SBA Home Page

FIGURE 8.11

Fast Company CoF
Page

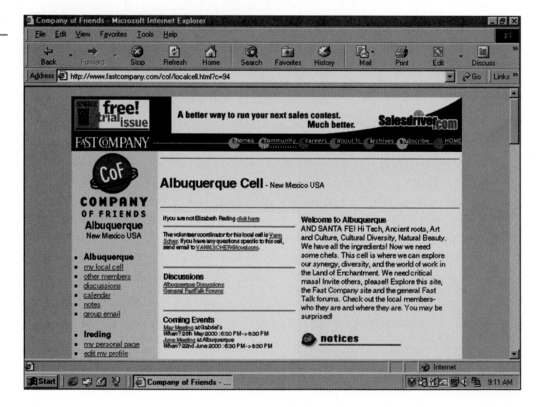

FIGURE 8.12

SOHO America Home Page

There is a lot more to running an eBusiness than writing business and marketing plans and designing a cool website. You need to understand the inner workings of your business through somewhat arduous tools such as accounting.

You also need to understand how to get the most from the people working with you. How can you effectively motivate them? How can you become an effective leader?

Some of your employees may be telecommuters. This new mode of working has its own positive and negative aspects.

financial accounting	expenses	materiality
management accounting	net income (or loss)	journalizing
asset	going concern	posting
liability	periodicity	chart of accounts
equity	conservatism	adjusted trial balance
owner's equity	realization	virtual organization
revenues	consistency	telecommuting

Complete the following statements:

1. _____ accounting is often used by people outside your organization.

2. Periodic reports that help employees make decisions are considered part of _____ accounting.

3. Something of value owned by the firm is called a(n) _____.

4. _____ are the inflow of assets resulting from the sale of goods or services.

5. Something owed by the firm is called a(n) _____.

6. The difference between revenues and expenses is called _____ income (or loss).

7. If you assume a company will remain in business, it is a _____ _____.

8. Having contingency plans and being pessimistic in estimates is called _____.

9. A geographically scattered group that communicates electronically and may never meet is called a(n) _____ _____.

10. Working from a remote location and communicating electronically is called _____.

Complete the following exercises:

1. Given your own accounting knowledge, define your areas of weakness and how additional information could be beneficial in a business environment.

2. Use your browser and your favorite search engine to locate three websites relevant to the type of eBusiness you would like to start. Print the home page for each of the sites.

Think of a leader you admire. This person can be well known or someone from your own experience. Write a one-page paper about the leadership qualities this person has that you find admirable and explain why.

Index

A

ABC News, 119
Accounting
    financial statements provided by, 148
    kinds of, 146–147
    knowledge of, 146–148
    procedures, 147–148
    terminology, 147
Accounting concepts, 147
ActiveX, 13
Adjusted trial balance, 147
Adobe Page Mill, 88
Adobe SiteMill, 88
Advertising, 39
Always-on Internet service, 23
Angels, 28
Annotating documents, 56
Applet, 13
Assets, 147

B

Balance sheet, 42
Bandwidth, 116–117
Barriers to entry, 58
Bed Bath and Beyond, 11–12
Board of directors, 40–41
Bookmarking, 14
Borders and colors, 132–133
Brick-and-mortar companies, 6
Browser, 13–15
    closing, 23
Bureaucracy, 149
Business description, 30–32
Business goals and needs, 4–6
Business law, 149
Business plan
    audience for, 28
    business description, 30–32
    executive summary, 28–30, 31
    financial considerations, 41–43
    footnotes/endnotes, 32
    market analysis, 34–36
    market position, 34
    mission statement, 32–33
    necessary ingredients, 29
    need for, 28
    pricing policy, 34
    product/service development, 36–38
    proposed products or services, 33–34
    sales and marketing strategies, 38–39
    staff needs, 40–41
Business-to-business commerce, 62
Business Week Online, 23

C

Capital requirements, 38
Cash flow statement, 42
Cell padding, 134
Cells, 128
Chart of accounts, 147
Claris Home page, 88
Clip art, 108–109
CNBC, 13, 14, 16
Coca-Cola, 7
Communication, 151
Competition, 35
Competitors, knowledge of, 52
Conservatism, 148
Consistency, 148
Corel NetPerfect, 89
Corporate climate, 54
Corporate structure, 149
Cost of goods, 38
Covey, Stephen, 149
Copyright laws, 112
Current employees, 28
Customer base, 34–35
Customers
    data mining, 78
    decision making by, 52
    demographics, 55
    in target market, 54–55

D

Data bandwidth, 116–117
Data mining, 78
Default, 72
Dell Computer, 13
Demographics, 55
Dial-up Internet service, 23
Digital cameras, 108

Directory, 18
Distribution channels, 39
Documents
    annotating, 56
    embedding comments in, 52, 53
    password protection, 50, 51

E

eBusiness, 4
    accounting, 145–148
    data gathering, 119
    financial statements, 148
    future concerns, 6
    goals and needs, 4–6
    Internet help sources, 155
    Internet identity, 9
    logo, 7
    mail client, 20–22
    main considerations, 5–6
    management techniques, 148–150
    telecommuting, 151–154
    virtual organizations, 151
eCommerce, 4
Economic entity, 148
Economy of motion, 40–41
E-mail, 20–22
    common tasks, 22
    creating, 22
Employees, current or potential, 28
Enabling software, 62
Endnotes, 32
entrepreneur.com, 53, 54
Equity, 147
Ethics, and Internet, 112
Eudora Pro mail client, 20, 21
Excite, 20
Executive summary
    for business plan, 28–30, 31
    for marketing plan, 49
Expenses, 147
External accounting, 146–147

F

Face time, 153
Fields, 119
Financial accounting, 146–147
Financial information, 38; *see also* Accounting
    balance sheet, 42
    capital requirements, 38
    cash flow statement, 42
    cost of goods, 38
    income statement, 42
    money needs, 42
    operating expenses, 38
    production costs, 37
    risk assessment, 41
Financial reporting, 147
Financial statements, 42, 148
Footnotes, 32
Formatting
    for graphic images, 108–109
    of tables, 130–132
    text, 69-72

Formatting toolbar, 71
Forms
    characteristics of, 119–120
    creating, 120–121
    design of, 78–79, 119-120
    finding, 119
    modifying, 121–123
Framed pages, 137–140
Frames
    controlling, 139
    use and design of, 135–136
Franklin Covey, 150

G

Gateway 2000, 13
Generally accepted accounting
            principles, 147
GlobalGold Internet Services, 150
Going concern, 148
Go Network, 16
Google, 30, 82
Go2Net, 17, 18
Graphic images
    commonly used formats, 109
    definition, 108
    format, 108–109
    inserting, 110–113
    obtaining, 110
    picture toolbar buttons, 113
Graphics design, 72–75
Graphics Interchange Format, 109

H

Handles, 99-100
Home office, 154–155
Home page, 7, 13
HotDog Pro, 88
HotMetal Pro, 89
Hotspot, 114
Hover button, 99-101
HTML (HyperText Markup Language)
    appearance of, 92–93
    definition, 11
    table tags, 129
Hyperlink dialog box, 115–116
Hyperlinks, 10–11, 114–116
    in tables, 129
    in websites, 140–141

I

Income statement, 42
Industry, 30–32
Industry outlook, 31–32
Industry position, 58
Informing, 61
Intellectual property, 112
Interactive website, 4–5
Internal accounting, 146–147

Internet
    browsers, 13–15
    help sources, 155
    piracy issue, 112
    portals, 15–18
Internet identity, 9

J–K

J. Jill, 39
Java, 13
Jennings, Peter, 119
Joint Photographic Experts Group, 109
Journalizing, 147
Key words, 18–19

L

Labor requirements, 37
Lawyers, 149
Leadership qualities, 149
Liabilities, 147, 149
List format, 98–99
Logo, 7
Lossy, 109
Lotus FastSite, 89
Lotus Notes, 20

M

Macintosh computers, 92
Mail client, 20–22
Management, 153
Management accounting, 147
Management staff, 40
Management techniques, 149
Managers, in telecommuting, 153
Market analysis
    customer base, 34–35
    defining competition, 35
    defining the market, 35
    estimated sales, 35–36
Marketing, 38–39
Marketing budget, 61–62
Marketing mix
    place, 61
    price, 60–61
    product, 60
    promotion, 61
Marketing plan
    advantages of products/services, 55–57
    budget, 61–62
    enabling software, 62
    executive summary, 49
    implementing, 63–64
    ingredients, 48–49
    need for, 48–49
    situational analysis, 50–54
    tactics, 58–61
    target market, 54–55
    uses, 48–49
Marketing tactics
    developmental considerations, 58

    marketing mix, 60–61
    pipeline, 58
Market position, 34
Market potential, 58
Market segments, 54
Materiality, 148
McGraw-Hill Companies, 9-10, 108
Mental disabilities, 82–83
Microsoft FrontPage, 90
    for adding graphics, 73–75
    color use, 75–78
    for creating forms, 120–121
    for creating framed pages, 137–140
    for creating links, 140–141
    for creating tables, 128–134
    for creating website, 80, 93–96
    for formatting text, 71–72
    for hover button, 99-101
    for inserting hyperlink, 114–116
    for list format, 98–99
    for modifying forms, 11–123
    for modifying web page, 96–98
    for navigation bar, 102–104
Microsoft Internet Explorer, 13–15
Microsoft mail client, 21
Microsoft Office, 20
Microsoft Outlook, 20
Microsoft Publisher, 89
    for creating websites, 80, 81
Microsoft Word, 30, 32, 50, 52
Mission statement, 32–33
Money needs, 42
Multimedia files, 116–118
Multimedia sites, 117–118

N

Navigation bar, 69, 102–104
Net income/loss, 147
Netscape Navigator, 13–15
Nike, Inc., 7
nolo.com, 146
Noninteractive website, 4–5

O

Object, 99-100
Operating expenses, 38
Osborne Media Group, 11
Owner's equity, 147
Ownership and control, 40

P

Padding, 134
Password protection, 50
PC Paintbrush, 109
Periodicity, 148
Personal liability, 149
Persuading, 61
Physical disabilities, 82–83

Picture file, 112
Pipeline, 58
Piracy problem, 112
Place, in marketing mix, 61
Popular opinion, 52
Portals, 15–18
    commonly available, 16
    comparison of, 16
    customizing, 17
    using, 16–17
Positioning, 57
Posting, 147
Potential demand, 52
Potential employees, 28
Previewing, 69
Price, in marketing mix, 60–61
Pricing policy, 34
Problem areas, 55–57
Product business, 4
    future concerns, 6
Production costs, 37
Production process, 36–37
Product life cycle, 58
Products, 33–34
Product/service, in marketing mix, 60
Product/service advantages
    industry position, 58
    problem areas, 55–57
Product/service development
    costs, 37
    financial information, 38
    labor requirements, 37
    meaning of, 36–37
    production process, 36–37
    prototype, 36
Promotion, 61
Prototypes, 36

R

Realization, 148
Reminders, 61
Revenues, 147
Risk assessment, 41

S

Sales, 38–39
Sales and marketing strategies, 38–39; *see also*
        Marketing plan
Sales estimation, 35–36
Scanner, 108
Search engines, 18–19
Search service, 18
Segments, 54
Service business, 4, 33–34; *see also*
        Product/service *entries*
    future concerns, 6
Situational analysis, 50–54
    corporate climate, 54
    defining competitors, 52
    effect of other organizations, 52

    potential demand, 52
    purchase decisions, 52
Small Business Administration,
        155, 156
Snap, 16
SOHO America Home Page, 157
Span, 128
Special-needs audience, 82–83
Staffing
    board of directors, 40–41
    management staff, 40
    ownership and control, 40
    support services, 41
Strategic partners, 28
Style, 96
Sundance, 39
Support services, 41

T

Table elements, 134
Tables
    with colors and borders, 132–133
    creating, 128–134
    with dialog box, 130
    formatting, 130–132
    with hyperlinks, 129
    uses, 128
Tagged Image File Format, 109
Tags, 92
Target market, 54–55
Taste, 69
Teams, 152–153
Telecommuting
    difficulties, 152
    from home office, 154–155
    interaction with manager, 153
    interaction with teammates, 152–153
    skills for, 151
Telecommuting equivalents, 154
Template, 94
Text
    alignment, 70
    attributes, 70
    font, 70
    formatting, 71–72
    style, 96
Theme, 75–76
Transactions, 147

U

UNIX, 92
URL (Uniform Resource Locator), 10–11

V

Venture capitalists, 28
Virtual organizations, 151
Virtual user groups, 155

W

Web, 93–96
Web-authoring tools, 88–91
Web editors, 88
Web page
    adding a hover button, 99-101
    adding a list, 98–99
    adding forms, 119–124
    closing, 23
    compared to website, 88
    components, 7–10
    in different browsers, 14–15
    framed, 135–140
    with graphic images, 108–114
    handles, 99-100
    inserting hyperlink, 114–116
    modifying, 96–98
    multimedia files, 116–118
    navigator bar, 102–104
    object, 99-100
    with tables, 128–134
    template, 94
Web page design
    creating forms, 78–79
    display issues, 70
    formatting text, 69-72
    good taste, 69
    with graphics, 72–75
    navigation bar, 69
    previewing, 69
    principles, 10
    resources, 81–82
    simplicity, 68
    for special-needs audience, 82–83
    theme, 75–76
    using color, 75–78
    white space, 68–69

Web presence
    definition, 6
    getting known, 6
Web session, ending, 23
Website
    bookmarking, 14
    created using FrontPage, 80
    created using MS Publisher, 81
    creating, 93–96
    HTML, 92–93
    including links, 140–141
    interactive or noninteractive, 4–5
    modifying a web page, 96–98
    planning, 88
    preliminary sketch, 89
    registering, 7
White space, 68–69
Windows Bitmap, 109
Windows Meta File, 109
Wizard, 80
World Wide Web
    always-on service, 23
    browsers, 13–15
    dial-up service, 23
    directory, 18
    ethics and, 112
    finding information on, 18–19
    key words, 18–19
    search engines, 18–19
    searching rules, 19
    search service, 18

Y

Yahoo!, 7, 16, 19